THE COMPLETE ANTI-INFLAMMATORY DIET FOR BEGINNERS

100 Healthy Recipes, Nutrition Guide, and A 7-Day Meal plan to Reduce Inflammation and Promote Wellness

Meghan Myers

Your Best Guide to Kick Start the Anti-Inflammatory Diet

TABLE OF CONTENTS

INTRODUCTION

Have you ever experienced pain or swelling after an injury or infection? That's your body's natural response to inflammation, which helps protect and heal the affected area. However, when inflammation becomes chronic, it can wreak havoc on your body and lead to a host of health problems.

The good news is that you can reduce chronic inflammation and improve your health by adopting an anti-inflammatory diet. This way of eating focuses on foods that are high in anti-inflammatory nutrients and low in pro-inflammatory nutrients, intending to reduce inflammation in the body.

This book will explore everything you need to know about anti-inflammatory diets. We'll cover the science behind inflammation and how chronic inflammation can contribute to health problems such as heart disease, cancer, and autoimmune disorders.

But don't worry; we won't use any complicated scientific jargon. We'll explain everything in plain English, so you can understand exactly what's happening in your body.

Next, we'll dive into what an anti-inflammatory diet is and how it can benefit your body. We'll talk about the foods to avoid and include in your diet and the many benefits of following this way of eating.

We'll also explore the science behind anti-inflammatory foods, including specific nutrients that reduce inflammation. We'll provide a detailed list of the best anti-inflammatory foods and explain why these foods are so good for your body.

But we won't just stop at food. We'll also provide practical tips and tools for meal planning and preparation, as well as supplement use and lifestyle changes that can help promote an anti-inflammatory lifestyle.

And to make things even easier, we've included 100 anti-inflammatory recipes, perfect for anyone looking to add more anti-inflammatory foods to their diet.

We aim to help you understand the importance of an anti-inflammatory diet and provide practical tips and tools for making this lifestyle change. We want to empower you to take control of your health and improve your overall well-being.

So, let's embark on this journey together and discover the world of anti-inflammatory eating. Let's learn, grow, and improve our health one bite at a time.

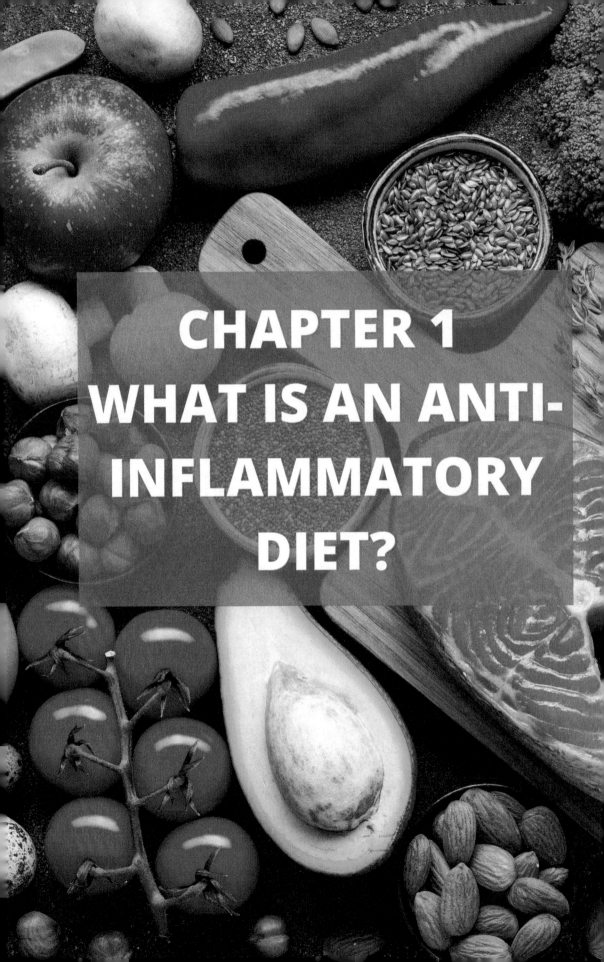

CHAPTER 1
WHAT IS AN ANTI-INFLAMMATORY DIET?

WHAT IS AN ANTI-INFLAMMATORY DIET AND HOW IT WORKS

Imagine waking up each morning feeling refreshed and energized. You step on the scale and notice that you've lost a few pounds, but more importantly, you feel healthier and happier than ever. What's your secret? An anti-inflammatory diet.

An anti-inflammatory diet is not just another fad diet or a quick fix. It is a way of life that promotes overall health and well-being. Inflammation is the body's natural response to injury or infection. However, when inflammation becomes chronic, it can lead to various health problems, including heart disease, arthritis, diabetes, and even cancer.

The good news is that we can control inflammation through our diet. An anti-inflammatory diet is all about eating whole, nutrient-dense foods rich in antioxidants, vitamins, and minerals. These foods help fight free radicals, unstable molecules that can cause inflammation and damage our cells.

So, what exactly does an anti-inflammatory diet consist of? It's simple. You should focus on eating plenty of fruits and vegetables, whole grains, lean proteins, and healthy fats. Foods high in refined sugar, saturated fat, and processed ingredients should be avoided, as they can trigger inflammation in the body.

You can think of an anti-inflammatory diet as a rainbow to make things more accessible. The more colorful your plate, the better. Brightly colored fruits and vegetables, such as blueberries, spinach, and sweet potatoes, are rich in antioxidants that help to reduce inflammation in the body.

Healthy fats, such as those found in nuts, seeds, and oily fish like salmon, are also essential for an anti-inflammatory diet. These fats help to reduce inflammation by promoting the production of anti-inflammatory compounds in the body.

In addition to eating the right foods, an anti-inflammatory diet involves lifestyle changes that promote overall health and well-being. This includes getting enough sleep, reducing stress, and exercising regularly.

An anti-inflammatory diet can improve your overall health and reduce your risk of chronic disease. It's a simple and effective way to take control of your health and well-being. So, start today by incorporating whole, nutrient-dense foods into your diet and making healthy lifestyle choices. Your body will thank you for it!

BENEFITS OF AN ANTI-INFLAMMATORY DIET

In the previous section, we discussed what an anti-inflammatory diet is and how it works. Now, let's dive into the many benefits of this type of eating plan.

1. **Reduces Chronic Inflammation:** As we mentioned before, chronic inflammation is linked to various health issues, such as heart disease, diabetes, and cancer. By following an anti-inflammatory diet, you can help to reduce inflammation in the body, which may lower the risk of these chronic diseases.
2. **Supports Weight Loss:** An anti-inflammatory diet emphasizes nutrient-dense, whole foods such as fruits, vegetables, and lean protein. These foods are often lower in calories than processed, high-fat foods, making them an excellent choice for those looking to lose weight.
3. **Improves Gut Health:** The gut plays a crucial role in the immune system, and a healthy gut is essential for overall health. An anti-inflammatory diet includes plenty of fiber-rich foods such as fruits, vegetables, and whole grains, promoting the growth of beneficial gut bacteria and supporting digestive health.
4. **Boosts Brain Function:** Inflammation has been linked to cognitive decline and neurological disorders such as Alzheimer's and Parkinson's. The anti-inflammatory foods in this diet, such as fatty fish, nuts, and berries, are rich in nutrients essential for brain health and function.
5. **Improves Heart Health:** By reducing inflammation, an anti-inflammatory diet can help lower the risk of heart disease. Additionally, many foods included in this diet, such as fatty fish, nuts, and olive oil, are rich in heart-healthy nutrients such as omega-3 fatty acids and monounsaturated fats.
6. **Helps Manage Autoimmune Conditions:** Autoimmune conditions occur when the immune system mistakenly attacks healthy cells in the body. Many of these conditions, such as rheumatoid arthritis and multiple sclerosis, are characterized by chronic inflammation. An anti-inflammatory diet may help to reduce inflammation and improve symptoms in those with autoimmune conditions.
7. **Promotes Healthy Aging:** Inflammation is thought to play a role in aging. An anti-inflammatory diet can help reduce inflammation and potentially slow the aging process.

In conclusion, there are many benefits to following an anti-inflammatory diet, including reducing chronic inflammation, supporting weight loss, improving gut health, boosting brain function, improving heart health, managing autoimmune conditions, and promoting healthy aging. You can improve your overall health and well-being by making simple changes to your diet and lifestyle.

FOODS TO AVOID ON AN ANTI-INFLAMMATORY DIET

One of the most effective ways to follow an anti-inflammatory diet is to know what foods to avoid. Many foods can cause inflammation, and reducing or eliminating these foods can have significant health benefits. This section will explore some common foods that should be avoided on an anti-inflammatory diet.

1. **Processed Foods:** Processed foods are often high in sugar, unhealthy fats, and preservatives that can cause inflammation. These foods include packaged snacks, fast food, frozen meals, and sugary drinks. Many processed foods also contain high amounts of refined carbohydrates, which can spike blood sugar levels and cause inflammation.
2. **Red Meat:** Red meat can be inflammatory, mainly when cooked at high temperatures. This is because the cooking process can produce advanced glycation end products (AGEs), which can contribute to inflammation in the body. It is best to limit or avoid red meat and opt for leaner protein sources like fish, poultry, and plant-based proteins.
3. **Fried Foods:** Fried foods are high in unhealthy fats and can cause inflammation. This includes fried chicken, French fries, onion rings, and other fried snacks. Avoiding these foods or choosing healthier alternatives like baked or grilled foods is best.
4. **Dairy Products:** Dairy products like milk, cheese, and yogurt can be inflammatory for some people. This is because dairy contains a protein called casein, which can be difficult for some people to digest. If you suspect that dairy is causing inflammation in your body, it may be best to eliminate it from your diet or switch to dairy alternatives like almond milk or soy milk.
5. **Gluten:** Gluten is a protein found in wheat, barley, and rye, which can be inflammatory for some people. This includes people with celiac disease or gluten sensitivity. If you suspect that gluten is causing inflammation in your body, it is best to avoid gluten-containing foods and opt for gluten-free alternatives.
6. **Alcohol:** Alcohol can cause inflammation in the body, particularly when consumed in large amounts. This is because alcohol can damage the gut lining, leading to inflammation and other health problems. It is best to limit alcohol consumption or avoid it altogether.

In summary, an anti-inflammatory diet involves avoiding or limiting foods that can cause inflammation. This includes processed, red meat, fried foods, dairy products, gluten, and alcohol. By making these dietary changes, you can reduce inflammation and improve your overall health and well-being.

FOODS TO INCLUDE IN AN ANTI-INFLAMMATORY DIET

Eating an anti-inflammatory diet is one of the most effective ways to reduce inflammation and improve overall health. An anti-inflammatory diet is rich in foods packed with nutrients, vitamins, and minerals that help reduce inflammation.

Here are 10 foods that you should include in your anti-inflammatory diet:

1. **Leafy Greens:** Leafy greens such as kale, spinach, and collard greens are packed with antioxidants, vitamins, and minerals that help to reduce inflammation in your body. These greens also contain high levels of fiber that help to support healthy digestion.
2. **Berries:** Berries such as blueberries, strawberries, and raspberries are high in antioxidants and phytonutrients that help to reduce inflammation in your body. Berries are also rich in fiber, which helps to support healthy digestion.
3. **Fatty Fish:** Fatty fish such as salmon, tuna, and sardines are rich in omega-3 fatty acids, which help to reduce inflammation in your body. These fish are also high in protein and other essential nutrients that help to support healthy muscle function.
4. **Nuts:** Nuts such as almonds, walnuts, and cashews are rich in healthy fats, vitamins, and minerals that help to reduce inflammation in your body. Nuts are also high in fiber and protein, which helps to support healthy digestion and muscle function.
5. **Olive Oil:** Olive oil is rich in monounsaturated fats, which help to reduce inflammation in your body. Olive oil is also packed with antioxidants and other essential nutrients that help to support overall health and well-being.
6. **Turmeric:** Turmeric is a spice that is commonly used in Indian cuisine. It contains a compound called curcumin, which has powerful anti-inflammatory properties. Adding turmeric to your meals or taking it as a supplement can help to reduce inflammation in your body.
7. **Ginger:** Ginger is another spice that is known for its anti-inflammatory properties. Adding ginger to your meals or drinking ginger tea can help to reduce inflammation and support healthy digestion.

- Garlic: Garlic is a member of the allium family and is known for its anti-inflammatory properties. Adding garlic to your meals can help to reduce inflammation and support overall health and well-being.
- Green Tea: Green tea is packed with antioxidants and phytonutrients that help to reduce inflammation in your body. Drinking green tea regularly can help to improve your overall health and well-being.
- Whole Grains: Whole grains such as brown rice, quinoa, and oats are high in fiber and other essential nutrients that help support healthy digestion and reduce inflammation.

Including these 10 foods in your anti-inflammatory diet can help reduce inflammation and improve your overall health and well-being. It's important to note that an anti-inflammatory diet is not a quick fix but a lifestyle change that requires consistent effort and dedication. You can improve your health and well-being in the long run by making minor changes to your diet and including more anti-inflammatory foods.

CHAPTER 2
THE SCIENCE BEHIND ANTI-INFLAMMATORY FOODS

THE SCIENCE BEHIND ANTI-INFLAMMATORY FOODS

Have you ever wondered how anti-inflammatory foods work? Let's dive into the science behind it.

Inflammation is a natural process in the body in response to injury, infection, or other irritants. However, chronic inflammation can lead to various health problems like heart disease, cancer, and autoimmune disorders.

Anti-inflammatory foods help to reduce inflammation in the body by blocking the production of pro-inflammatory compounds. These compounds, such as cytokines and prostaglandins, can cause inflammation and tissue damage when produced in excess.

Certain nutrients in anti-inflammatory foods have been shown to have a significant impact on reducing inflammation. For example, omega-3 fatty acids found in fish, nuts, and seeds are known to decrease inflammation by suppressing the production of pro-inflammatory compounds.

Similarly, antioxidants found in fruits and vegetables can reduce inflammation by neutralizing free radicals that damage cells and contribute to inflammation. Examples of antioxidant-rich foods include berries, leafy greens, and tomatoes.

Other anti-inflammatory foods include ginger, turmeric, garlic, and green tea. These foods contain natural compounds that have been shown to reduce inflammation and provide a wide range of other health benefits.

Incorporating more anti-inflammatory foods into your diet can reduce chronic inflammation and improve overall health. Remember, it's essential to eat a balanced diet and talk to your healthcare provider before significantly changing your diet or lifestyle.

ANTI-INFLAMMATORY NUTRIENTS AND THEIR HEALTH BENEFITS

When it comes to eating an anti-inflammatory diet, one of the most important things to remember is the importance of consuming specific nutrients that have been shown to have potent anti-inflammatory properties. This section will discuss some critical nutrients in anti-inflammatory foods and their health benefits.

- **Omega-3 Fatty Acids:** Omega-3 fatty acids are a type of healthy fat shown to have potent anti-inflammatory effects. These fats are found in fatty fish (salmon, sardines, and mackerel), flaxseed, chia seeds, and walnuts. Studies have linked a higher intake of omega-3s to a lower risk of chronic diseases such as heart disease, diabetes, and certain types of cancer.
- **Fiber:** Fiber is a type of carbohydrate that is found in plant-based foods like fruits, vegetables, whole grains, and legumes. Eating a diet rich in fiber has been linked to a reduced risk of chronic diseases like heart disease and type 2 diabetes, as well as lower levels of inflammation in the body.
- **Vitamin D:** Vitamin D is an essential nutrient that helps the body absorb calcium and maintain healthy bones. Recent research has also shown that vitamin D has anti-inflammatory effects. Low vitamin D levels have been linked to an increased risk of chronic diseases like cancer and heart disease. Foods high in vitamin D include fatty fish, egg yolks, and fortified dairy products.
- **Antioxidants:** Antioxidants are a group of compounds that help protect the body against damage caused by free radicals, which are harmful molecules that can contribute to inflammation and chronic disease. Some common antioxidants include vitamins A, C, and E, selenium, and beta-carotene. These nutrients can be found in foods like berries, citrus fruits, leafy greens, nuts, and seeds.
- **Probiotics:** Probiotics are beneficial bacteria that live in the gut and play an essential role in overall health. These bacteria have been shown to help reduce inflammation, improve digestion, and boost the immune system. Probiotics can be found in fermented foods like yogurt, kefir, and sauerkraut.

Incorporating these essential nutrients into your diet can be a powerful way to support your body's natural anti-inflammatory processes and reduce your risk of chronic disease. Eating various colorful fruits and vegetables, lean proteins, healthy fats, and whole grains give your body the nutrients it needs to function at its best.

THE LINK BETWEEN INFLAMMATION AND CHRONIC DISEASES

Inflammation is a natural response of the body's immune system to protect against harmful stimuli such as infections, injuries, or toxins. However, when this response becomes chronic, it can lead to several chronic diseases, including cancer, diabetes, heart disease, and autoimmune disorders.

When inflammation becomes chronic, it can cause damage to tissues and organs, leading to the development of chronic diseases. For instance, chronic inflammation can cause damage to the inner lining of blood vessels, leading to plaque buildup and, eventually, heart disease. Similarly, chronic inflammation can damage the insulin-producing cells in the pancreas, leading to insulin resistance and diabetes.

Moreover, chronic inflammation can also contribute to the development of cancer. Inflammation causes DNA damage, which can lead to the mutation of cells and, eventually, cancer. Inflammation also plays a role in the growth and spread of cancer cells by creating an environment that promotes survival.

Autoimmune disorders such as rheumatoid arthritis, lupus, and multiple sclerosis are also linked to chronic inflammation. In these conditions, the immune system mistakenly attacks the body's tissues, leading to chronic inflammation and tissue damage.

It is essential to control chronic inflammation to reduce the risk of chronic diseases. An anti-inflammatory diet rich in whole foods, fruits, vegetables, and healthy fats can help reduce inflammation. Regular exercise, stress management, and getting enough sleep are essential in controlling chronic inflammation.

In conclusion, chronic inflammation is a leading contributor to the development of several chronic diseases. By understanding the link between inflammation and chronic diseases and adopting healthy lifestyle choices, we can reduce the risk of developing these conditions and lead a more healthy life.

hello

What do you think of this cookbook?

If you can spare two minutes to write a review on Amazon, it will help many other shoppers make the right decision.

CHAPTER 3
ANTI-INFLAMMATORY MEAL PLANNING

TIPS FOR PLANNING ANTI-INFLAMMATORY MEALS

Planning anti-inflammatory meals doesn't have to be complicated or overwhelming. With a few simple tips, you can create delicious and healthy meals that help reduce inflammation.

First, focus on incorporating whole foods into your meals. This means choosing fresh fruits and vegetables, whole grains, and lean protein sources like chicken or fish. These foods are rich in nutrients and antioxidants that can help combat inflammation and promote overall health.

Next, pay attention to your plate proportions. Fill half of your plate with non-starchy vegetables, like leafy greens, broccoli, or bell peppers. Then, allocate a quarter of your plate for lean protein and another quarter for whole grains or starchy vegetables, like sweet potatoes or brown rice. This balance of nutrients can help keep you full and satisfied while supporting anti-inflammatory processes in your body.

Another critical aspect of planning anti-inflammatory meals is being mindful of your cooking methods. Instead of deep-frying or pan-frying your food, try grilling, baking, or steaming. These methods can help preserve your food's nutrients while reducing the amount of added oils or fats.

Finally, don't forget to add some healthy fats to your meals. Foods like avocados, nuts, and olive oil contain healthy monounsaturated and polyunsaturated fats that can help reduce inflammation. Just be sure to enjoy them in moderation, as they are still a source of calories.

By incorporating these tips into your meal planning, you can create delicious and healthy meals that support an anti-inflammatory lifestyle.

7-DAY MEAL PLAN

Day	Breakfast	Lunch	Snack	Dinner
1	Breakfast Hash	Tuna Salad	Greek Yogurt with Berries	Chicken and Vegetable Stir-Fry
2	Oatmeal with Apples and Walnuts	Chicken and Vegetable Stir-Fry	Hummus and Carrot Sticks	Broiled Salmon with Asparagus
3	Spinach and Mushroom Omelette	Quinoa Salad with Roasted Vegetables	Hard Boiled Egg	Turkey and Sweet Potato Chili
4	Sweet Potato and Black Bean Breakfast Skillet	Greek Salad with Grilled Chicken	Almond Butter and Banana	Lemon Herb Roasted Chicken with Roasted Broccoli
5	Banana Nut Smoothie	Zucchini Noodle Pad Thai	Apple Slices with Almond Butter	Turkey Burgers with Sweet Potato Fries
6	Blueberry Chia Pudding	Lentil Soup	Hummus and Celery	Baked Cod with Asparagus
7	Avocado Toast with Smoked Salmon	Quinoa and Black Bean Salad	Mixed Nuts	Beef and Vegetable Stir-Fry

CHAPTER 4
ANTI-INFLAMMATORY SUPPLEMENTS

ANTI-INFLAMMATORY SUPPLEMENTS AND THEIR HEALTH BENEFITS

Recently, many people have turned to supplements to improve their health and reduce inflammation. Anti-inflammatory supplements are becoming increasingly popular, and for a good reason. These supplements can offer a range of health benefits and can help people maintain a healthy lifestyle.

One of the most popular anti-inflammatory supplements is Omega-3 fatty acids. These are essential fatty acids that our bodies cannot produce alone. Omega-3s have been shown to reduce inflammation in the body and improve heart health. They are found in foods such as salmon, mackerel, and chia seeds, but many people take supplements to ensure they get enough.

Another popular anti-inflammatory supplement is turmeric. Turmeric is a spice commonly used in Indian cuisine, and it contains a compound called curcumin. Curcumin has been shown to have anti-inflammatory properties and may help reduce the risk of certain diseases. Many people take turmeric supplements to get a higher dose of curcumin than they would get from eating turmeric in their food.

Probiotics are another anti-inflammatory supplement that has gained popularity in recent years. Probiotics are live bacteria and yeasts that are good for your digestive system. They can help reduce inflammation in the gut and improve digestion. Probiotics can be found in foods such as yogurt, but many people take supplements to get enough.

Vitamin D is another supplement that has been shown to have anti-inflammatory properties. Our bodies produce vitamin D when exposed to sunlight, but many people don't get enough sun exposure alone. Vitamin D can also be found in foods such as fatty fish and fortified milk, but supplements are a popular choice for deficient people.

In addition to these supplements, many others have been shown to have anti-inflammatory properties, such as ginger, green tea, and resveratrol. It's important to note, however, that supplements are not a replacement for a healthy diet and lifestyle. Eating various whole foods and exercising regularly is essential to maintain good health.

In conclusion, anti-inflammatory supplements can offer a range of health benefits and help reduce inflammation in the body. Omega-3 fatty acids, turmeric, probiotics, and vitamin D, are just a few examples of effective popular supplements. However, it's important to remember that supplements do not replace a healthy lifestyle. Eating various whole foods and exercising regularly is essential to maintain good health.

WARNINGS AND PRECAUTIONS

While supplements can offer a range of health benefits, it is vital to be aware of any potential risks and precautions associated with their use. Some general considerations to keep in mind when taking supplements include:

1. **Consult your healthcare provider:** Before taking any new supplement, it is always a good idea to consult with your healthcare provider. They can help you determine whether a supplement is appropriate for you and guide you on dosing and potential interactions with any medications you are taking.
2. **Be cautious with dosage:** Taking more than the recommended supplement can be tempting to achieve faster results. However, this can be dangerous and potentially harmful. Always stick to the recommended dosage on the supplement label or as your healthcare provider advises.
3. **Be aware of potential interactions:** Supplements can interact with other medications and supplements, potentially leading to adverse effects. Always inform your healthcare provider about any supplements you are taking, and avoid taking multiple supplements containing the same ingredients.
4. **Choose reputable brands:** Not all supplements are equal; some may contain harmful ingredients or toxins. Look for supplements from reputable brands tested for purity and quality.
5. **Be cautious with herbal supplements:** While many can offer health benefits, they can also be powerful and potentially harmful. Be sure to research any herbal supplements before taking them, and be especially cautious if you are pregnant or breastfeeding.
6. **Watch for side effects:** While many supplements are generally safe when taken as directed, some can cause side effects such as nausea, headaches, or digestive issues. If you experience any unusual symptoms after starting a new supplement, stop taking it and consult with your healthcare provider.

Following these guidelines and being cautious when taking supplements can help you get the most benefit while minimizing potential risks or side effects.

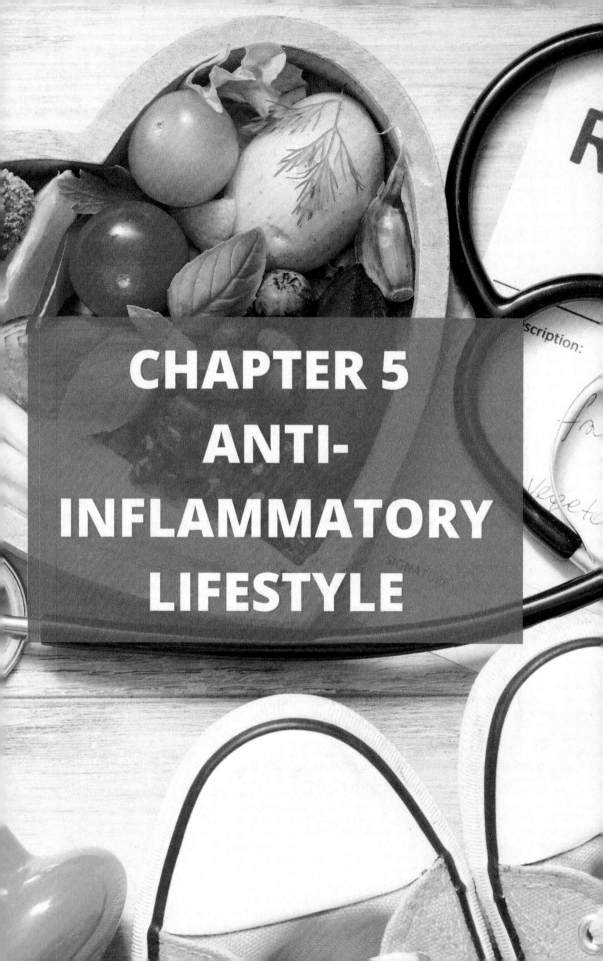

CHAPTER 5
ANTI-INFLAMMATORY LIFESTYLE

LIFESTYLE CHANGES THAT CAN HELP REDUCE INFLAMMATION

Various factors such as stress, lack of exercise, smoking, and a poor diet can cause inflammation. Fortunately, changing your lifestyle can help reduce inflammation and improve your overall health.

1. **Diet:** A healthy and balanced diet is one of the most effective ways to reduce inflammation. Focus on consuming plenty of fruits and vegetables, whole grains, lean proteins, and healthy fats. Avoid processed and fried foods, as well as sugar and artificial sweeteners. Additionally, limiting or eliminating alcohol and caffeine can also help reduce inflammation.
2. **Exercise:** Regular physical activity can help reduce inflammation by improving circulation and promoting the release of anti-inflammatory compounds. Aim for at least 30 minutes of moderate-intensity exercise, such as brisk walking or cycling, most days of the week.
3. **Stress management:** Chronic stress can contribute to inflammation, so finding healthy ways to manage stress is crucial. This could include meditation, yoga, deep breathing exercises, or spending time in nature.
4. **Sleep:** Getting enough sleep is essential for reducing inflammation, as sleep deprivation has been linked to increased inflammation in the body. Aim for 7-8 hours of sleep each night and establish a regular sleep routine.
5. **Quitting smoking:** Smoking is a significant source of inflammation in the body, and quitting smoking is essential to reducing inflammation and improving overall health.
6. **Maintaining a healthy weigh**t: Excess weight, especially around the waist, is associated with increased inflammation in the body. Maintaining a healthy weight through a healthy diet and regular exercise can help reduce inflammation and improve overall health.

By making these lifestyle changes, individuals can help reduce inflammation and improve overall health. These changes can be challenging but worth it in the long run for their numerous health benefits.

TIPS FOR STRESS REDUCTION AND BETTER SLEEP

Stress and lack of sleep are the most significant contributors to chronic inflammation. By reducing stress and improving the quality of your sleep, you can significantly decrease your body's inflammatory response. Here are some tips to help you achieve this:

1. **Practice relaxation techniques:** Deep breathing, meditation, and yoga are all great ways to relax and reduce stress. Make time for these activities each day, even just a few minutes.
2. **Exercise regularly:** Exercise not only helps to reduce stress, but it also helps to improve sleep quality. Aim for at least 30 minutes of moderate-intensity exercise each day.
3. **Limit caffeine and alcohol**: Both caffeine and alcohol can disrupt sleep and increase stress levels. Limit your consumption of these substances, especially in the evening.
4. **Create a sleep-friendly environment:** Ensure your bedroom is calm, dark, and quiet. Use comfortable bedding and invest in a good quality mattress and pillows.
5. **Stick to a sleep schedule:** Try to go to bed and wake up simultaneously each day, even on weekends. This helps to regulate your body's sleep-wake cycle.
6. **Practice good sleep hygiene:** Avoid screens for at least an hour before bedtime, avoid heavy meals and strenuous exercise close to rest, and establish a relaxing bedtime routine.
7. **Get sunlight exposure:** Sunlight during the day can help regulate your body's natural sleep-wake cycle and improve sleep quality. Try to spend time outside daily, even just a few minutes.
8. **Consider natural remedies:** Certain herbs and supplements, such as valerian root, chamomile, and magnesium, can help promote relaxation and improve sleep quality. Consult with your healthcare provider before starting any new supplements.

By incorporating these tips into your daily routine, you can reduce stress and improve the quality of your sleep, which can have a significant impact on reducing inflammation in the body.

EXERCISE RECOMMENDATIONS

Exercise is an essential component of an anti-inflammatory lifestyle. It has been shown to reduce inflammation, improve mood, and enhance overall health. The following are some exercise recommendations for an anti-inflammatory lifestyle:

1. **Aerobic exercise**: This type of exercise reduces inflammation and improves overall health. Aerobic exercise includes walking, jogging, cycling, swimming, and dancing. Aiming for at least 150 minutes of moderate-intensity aerobic exercise or 75 minutes of vigorous aerobic activity per week is recommended.

2. **Resistance training:** Resistance training, also known as strength training, is vital for building and maintaining muscle mass, which can help reduce inflammation. Resistance training includes lifting weights, using resistance bands, and bodyweight exercises. Aiming for at least two days per week of resistance training is recommended, targeting all major muscle groups.

3. **High-intensity interval training (HIIT):** HIIT involves short bursts of high-intensity activity followed by rest periods. It has been shown to improve cardiovascular health, reduce inflammation, and enhance overall fitness. HIIT can be performed using a variety of activities such as running, cycling, or bodyweight exercises.

4. **Yoga and stretching:** Yoga and stretching are great for reducing stress and improving flexibility. These types of exercises can also help reduce inflammation and improve overall health. Incorporating yoga or stretching into your exercise routine can be a great way to enhance your anti-inflammatory lifestyle.

5. **Daily activity**: Besides structured exercise, everyday activities such as walking, taking the stairs, and doing household chores can also help reduce inflammation and improve overall health. Aim to be as active as possible throughout the day and avoid prolonged periods of sitting or inactivity.

Consider a healthcare professional before starting any new exercise routine, especially if you have pre-existing health conditions. By incorporating these exercise recommendations into your daily routine, you can enhance your anti-inflammatory lifestyle and improve your overall health.

CHAPTER 6
BREAKFAST

AVOCADO AND EGG BREAKFAST SANDWICH

5 minutes   10 minutes   1

Ingredients

- 1 large egg
- 1 slice of whole-grain bread
- 1/4 of a ripe avocado, mashed
- 1/4 teaspoon of ground cumin
- 1/4 teaspoon of ground coriander
- 1/4 teaspoon of smoked paprika
- 1/4 teaspoon of garlic powder
- Salt and pepper to taste (optional)

Preparation Steps

- Preheat a non-stick skillet over medium heat.
- Mix the mashed avocado, cumin, coriander, smoked paprika, garlic powder, and a pinch of salt and pepper in a small bowl.
- Toast the bread until golden brown and set aside.
- Crack the egg into the skillet and season with salt and pepper. Cook for 2-3 minutes until the white is set and the yolk is still runny.
- Spread the avocado mixture onto the toasted bread and top with the cooked egg.
- Serve immediately.

Calories: 315kcal | Carbohydrates: 21g | Protein: 13g | Fat: 21g | Saturated Fat: 4g | Cholesterol: 186mg | Sodium: 291mg | Fiber: 8g | Sugar: 1g

This breakfast sandwich provides a healthy dose of protein, fiber, and healthy fats from avocado and whole-grain bread. The spices used in the avocado spread also contain anti-inflammatory properties. The recipe can easily be scaled up to serve more people by increasing the number of ingredients. Enjoy!

BERRY AND CHIA SEED PUDDING

5 minutes   5 minutes   2

Ingredients

- 1/4 cup of chia seeds
- 1 cup of unsweetened almond milk
- 1/2 tsp of vanilla extract
- 1/2 tsp of ground cinnamon
- 1/2 cup of mixed berries (fresh or frozen)
- 1 tbsp of honey or maple syrup (optional)

Preparation Steps

- Whisk together chia seeds, almond milk, vanilla extract, and cinnamon in a medium-sized bowl. If using a sweetener, add it now and whisk until combined.
- Cover the bowl and refrigerate for at least 4 hours or overnight until the chia seeds have absorbed the liquid and the mixture has thickened to a pudding-like consistency.
- When ready to serve, divide the pudding into two bowls and top each with the mixed berries.
- Serve immediately and enjoy!

Calories: 147kcal | Carbohydrates: 17g | Protein: 4g | Fat: 8g | Saturated Fat: 1g | Sodium: 92mg | Fiber: 9g | Sugar: 6g

This delicious and nutritious Berry and Chia Seed Pudding is a perfect anti-inflammatory breakfast or snack. Chia seeds are an excellent omega-3 fatty acids, fiber, and protein source, while berries are rich in antioxidants and other anti-inflammatory compounds. The recipe is easily adaptable by using different types of milk and toppings, such as sliced almonds or shredded coconut. Enjoy this healthy and tasty pudding!

BLUEBERRY OATMEAL BAKE
10 minutes   35 minutes   4

Ingredients

- 1 cup of rolled oats
- 1/4 cup of chopped nuts (such as almonds or walnuts)
- 1/4 cup of unsweetened shredded coconut
- 1 tsp of ground cinnamon
- 1/4 tsp of salt
- 1 cup of unsweetened almond milk
- 1/4 cup of pure maple syrup
- 1 large egg
- 1 tsp of vanilla extract
- 1 cup of fresh or frozen blueberries

Preparation Steps

- Preheat the oven to 350°F (175°C).
- Combine rolled oats, chopped nuts, shredded coconut, cinnamon, and salt in a large bowl.
- Whisk together almond milk, maple syrup, egg, and vanilla extract in a separate bowl.
- Add the wet ingredients to the dry ingredients and stir until well combined.
- Fold in the blueberries.
- Pour the mixture into a greased 8x8-inch baking dish and smooth the top with a spatula.
- Bake for 35-40 minutes, until the edges are golden brown and the center is set.
- Let the oatmeal bake cool for a few minutes before serving. Serve warm, and enjoy!

Calories: 315kcal | Carbohydrates: 21g | Protein: 13g | Fat: 21g | Saturated Fat: 4g | Cholesterol: 186mg | Sodium: 291mg | Fiber: 8g | Sugar: 1g

This Blueberry Oatmeal Bake is a comforting and satisfying breakfast option packed with fiber, protein, and healthy fats. The oats and nuts provide slow-burning carbohydrates, while the blueberries add flavor and antioxidants. The recipe can easily be doubled to serve a larger group or to have leftovers for the week. Serve with a dollop of Greek yogurt and a drizzle of maple syrup for an extra touch of sweetness. Enjoy!

COCONUT FLOUR PANCAKES

10 minutes   10 minutes   2-3

Ingredients

- 1/2 cup of coconut flour
- 1/2 tsp of baking powder
- 1/4 tsp of salt
- 4 large eggs
- 1/2 cup of almond milk
- 2 tbsp of coconut oil, melted
- 1 tbsp of honey (optional)
- 1/2 tsp of vanilla extract
- Fresh fruit for topping
- Honey, for drizzling

Preparation Steps

- Whisk together coconut flour, baking powder, and salt in a large bowl.
- Whisk together eggs, almond milk, melted coconut oil, honey (if using), and vanilla extract in a separate bowl.
- Add the wet ingredients to the dry ingredients and stir until well combined. The mixture will be thick, but if it seems too thick, add almond milk.
- Heat a non-stick pan over medium heat and lightly coat with coconut oil or cooking spray.
- Spoon about 1/4 cup of batter onto the pan for each pancake.
- Cook for 2-3 minutes on each side until golden brown.
- Repeat with the remaining batter, greasing the pan as needed.
- Serve the pancakes topped with fresh fruit and a drizzle of honey.

Calories: 252kcal | Carbohydrates: 14g | Protein: 11g | Fat: 18g | Saturated Fat: 11g | Cholesterol: 186mg | Sodium: 339mg | Fiber: 7g | Sugar: 6g

These Coconut Flour Pancakes are a delicious and nutritious gluten-free breakfast option. Coconut flour is high in fiber and low in carbohydrates, making it an excellent alternative to traditional flour. Adding eggs and almond milk adds protein, while coconut oil provides healthy fats. Top the pancakes with your favorite fresh fruit and a drizzle of honey for added sweetness. Enjoy!

GREEK YOGURT PARFAIT

🌿 10 minutes ⏱ 0 minutes 🍴 2

Ingredients

- 1/2 cup of fresh mixed berries (such as blueberries, raspberries, and strawberries)
- 1 cup of plain Greek yogurt
- 1/2 cup of granola
- 1 tbsp of honey (optional)

Preparation Steps

- Start by adding a spoonful of yogurt to the bottom of each serving glass.
- Layer the berries on top of the yogurt, followed by a layer of granola.
- Repeat the layers until you reach the top of the glass.
- Drizzle honey over the top, if desired.
- Serve immediately or store in the fridge until ready to eat.

Calories: 240kcal | Carbohydrates: 33g | Protein: 17g | Fat: 5g | Saturated Fat: 1g | Cholesterol: 7mg | Sodium: 80mg | Fiber: 5g | Sugar: 17g

This Greek Yogurt Parfait is a delicious, healthy breakfast with protein, fiber and antioxidants. Greek yogurt provides a creamy and tangy base, while the fresh berries add sweetness and color. Granola adds crunch and fiber, and a drizzle of honey adds sweetness. This parfait can be easily customized using your favorite fruit and granola flavors. Enjoy!

MATCHA GREEN TEA SMOOTHIE

5 minutes   0 minutes   1

Ingredients

- 1 tsp of matcha green tea powder
- 1 cup of unsweetened almond milk
- 1/2 cup of frozen mixed berries
- 1/2 frozen banana
- 1 tbsp of honey (optional)

Preparation Steps

- Add all ingredients to a blender and blend until smooth and creamy.
- If the smoothie is too thick, add almond milk to thin it out.
- Pour the smoothie into a glass and enjoy immediately.

Calories: 150kcal | Carbohydrates: 28g | Protein: 3g | Fat: 4g | Saturated Fat: 0.3g | Cholesterol: 0mg | Sodium: 195mg | Fiber: 5g | Sugar: 18g

This Matcha Green Tea Smoothie is a delicious, energizing breakfast option packed with antioxidants, fiber, and vitamins. Matcha green tea powder provides a natural source of caffeine and antioxidants, while mixed berries and bananas add natural sweetness and vitamins. Unsweetened almond milk provides a creamy and dairy-free base, and honey can be added for extra sweetness if desired. This smoothie is a great way to start your day with a refreshing and nutritious boost!

QUINOA BREAKFAST BOWL
5 minutes   25 minutes   2

Ingredients

- 1/2 cup of quinoa
- 1 cup of water
- 2 cups of mixed greens
- 1 ripe avocado, sliced
- 2 soft-boiled eggs
- 2 tbsp of extra-virgin olive oil
- 2 tbsp of lemon juice
- Salt and pepper to taste (optional)

Preparation Steps

- Rinse the quinoa in a fine mesh strainer and place it in a medium-sized pot with the water.
- Bring to a boil over medium-high heat, then reduce the heat to low and simmer for 15-20 minutes, or until the water has been absorbed and the quinoa is tender.
- While the quinoa cooks, wash and dry the mixed greens and slice the avocado.
- Whisk together the extra-virgin olive oil, lemon juice, salt, and pepper in a small bowl to make the dressing.
- Once the quinoa is done cooking, divide it between two bowls.
- Top each bowl with mixed greens, sliced avocado, and a soft-boiled egg.
- Drizzle the dressing over each bowl, and enjoy!

Calories: 378kcal | Carbohydrates: 25g | Protein: 11g | Fat: 28g | Saturated Fat: 4g | Cholesterol: 186mg | Sodium: 62mg | Fiber: 8g | Sugar: 2g

This Quinoa Breakfast Bowl is a satisfying, nutritious breakfast with protein, fiber, and healthy fats. Quinoa provides a protein-packed base, while mixed greens and avocado add fiber and healthy fats. Soft-boiled eggs provide additional protein and nutrients, and a simple dressing made with extra-virgin olive oil and lemon juice adds flavor and healthy fats. This breakfast bowl is customizable and can quickly adapt to your taste by adding different vegetables or protein sources. Enjoy!

SWEET POTATO HASH
10 minutes   🕐 25 minutes   🍴 4

Ingredients

- 2 sweet potatoes, peeled and diced
- 1 yellow onion, diced
- 1 red bell pepper, seeded and diced
- 2 cloves of garlic, minced
- 1 tsp of turmeric powder
- 1 tsp of ginger powder
- 1/2 tsp of paprika
- Salt and pepper to taste (optional)
- 2 tbsp of extra-virgin olive oil
- 4 eggs

Preparation Steps

- Preheat the oven to 400°F (200°C).
- Combine the sweet potatoes, red bell pepper, yellow onion, garlic, turmeric powder, ginger powder, paprika, salt, pepper, and extra-virgin olive oil in a large bowl. Toss to combine.
- Transfer the sweet potato mixture to a baking sheet lined with parchment paper and spread it in an even layer.
- Roast in the oven for 20-25 minutes or until the sweet potatoes are tender and golden brown.
- While the sweet potato hash is cooking, cook the eggs to your desired doneness (fried, poached, or scrambled).
- Serve the sweet potato hash in bowls with the cooked eggs on top.

Calories: 257kcal | Carbohydrates: 25g | Protein: 9g | Fat: 14g | Saturated Fat: 3g | Cholesterol: 164mg | Sodium: 119mg | Fiber: 5g | Sugar: 7g

This Sweet Potato Hash is a hearty, filling breakfast option packed with anti-inflammatory spices like turmeric and ginger, fiber-rich sweet potatoes, and bell peppers. It is easy to make and can be customized to your taste preferences by adding different vegetables or adjusting the spices. Adding eggs provides protein and healthy fats, making it a well-rounded breakfast option. Enjoy!

TOFU SCRAMBLE

10 minutes   10 minutes   4

Ingredients

- 1 block of firm tofu, drained and crumbled
- 1 red bell pepper, seeded and diced
- 1 yellow onion, diced
- 1 cup of kale or spinach, chopped
- 2 cloves of garlic, minced
- 1 tsp of ground turmeric
- 1/2 tsp of ground cumin
- Salt and pepper to taste (optional)
- 2 tbsp of olive oil

Preparation Steps

- Heat the olive oil in a large skillet over medium heat.
- Add the onion and bell pepper, and sauté for 3-5 minutes, or until the vegetables are softened.
- Add the garlic, turmeric, cumin, salt, and pepper and combine.
- Add the crumbled tofu to the skillet and stir to combine with the vegetables and spices.
- Cook for 5-7 minutes or until the tofu is heated through and has absorbed the flavors of the spices and vegetables.
- Add the chopped kale or spinach to the skillet and stir to combine. Cook for 1-2 minutes or until the greens are wilted and tender.
- If desired, serve the tofu scramble hot, garnished with additional herbs or spices.

Calories: 122kcal | Carbohydrates: 6g | Protein: 8g | Fat: 8g | Saturated Fat: 1g | Sodium: 5mg | Fiber: 1g | Sugar: 2g

This Tofu Scramble is a vegan and protein-packed breakfast option perfect for those looking to incorporate more plant-based meals into their diet. The combination of tofu and vegetables provides a variety of nutrients and fiber while anti-inflammatory spices like turmeric and cumin add flavor and health benefits. Serve this scramble with whole grain toast or fresh fruit for a well rounded breakfast. Enjoy!

ZUCCHINI AND FETA FRITTATA

10 minutes   25 minutes   4

Ingredients

- 6 large eggs
- 1/2 cup of crumbled feta cheese
- 1 medium zucchini, grated
- 1/2 small onion, diced
- 1 clove of garlic, minced
- 1 tbsp of chopped fresh oregano
- 1 tsp of chopped fresh thyme
- Salt and pepper to taste (optional)
- 2 tbsp of olive oil

Preparation Steps

- Preheat the oven to 375°F (190°C).
- In a large bowl, whisk the eggs with the feta cheese, grated zucchini, diced onion, minced garlic, chopped oregano, chopped thyme, salt, and pepper.
- Heat the olive oil in a 10-inch oven-safe skillet over medium heat.
- Pour the egg mixture into the skillet and cook for 5-7 minutes or until the edges of the frittata begin to set.
- Transfer the skillet to the preheated oven and bake for 10-12 minutes, until the frittata is set and golden brown on top.
- Remove the skillet from the oven and let the frittata cool for a few minutes before slicing and serving.

Calories: 203kcal | Carbohydrates: 3g | Protein: 12g | Fat: 16g | Saturated Fat: 6g | Sodium: 382mg | Fiber: 1g | Sugar: 2g

This Zucchini and Feta Frittata is a delicious and savory breakfast option for those following an anti-inflammatory diet. Combining zucchini and feta cheese provides a satisfying and flavorful base, while anti-inflammatory herbs like oregano and thyme add taste and health benefits. Serve this frittata with fresh fruit or a simple green salad for a balanced and nutritious breakfast. Enjoy!

CHAPTER 7
LUNCH

GRILLED SALMON SALAD

🌿 10 minutes   ⏱ 10 minutes   🍽 4

Ingredients

- 4 (4-6 oz) salmon fillets, skin on
- 6 cups of mixed greens
- 1 avocado, sliced
- 1/2 cup of chopped walnuts
- 1/4 cup of crumbled feta cheese
- 1/4 cup of olive oil
- 2 tbsp of lemon juice
- 1 tbsp of Dijon mustard
- 1 clove of garlic, minced
- Salt and pepper to taste (optional

Preparation Steps

- Preheat a grill or grill pan to medium-high heat.
- Season the salmon fillets with salt and pepper.
- Place the salmon fillets skin-side down on the grill and cook for 3-4 minutes per side until cooked.
- Toss the mixed greens, sliced avocado, chopped walnuts, and crumbled feta cheese in a large bowl.
- Whisk together the olive oil, lemon juice, Dijon mustard, minced garlic, salt, and pepper in a small bowl.
- Pour the dressing over the salad and toss to combine.
- Divide the salad among four plates and top each with a grilled salmon fillet

Calories: 418kcal | Carbohydrates: 10g | Protein: 29g | Fat: 30g | Saturated Fat: 5g | Sodium: 177mg | Fiber: 6g | Sugar: 2g

This Grilled Salmon Salad is a flavorful and nutritious meal for lunch or dinner. The grilled salmon provides a healthy source of protein and omega-3 fatty acids, while the mixed greens, avocado, and walnuts offer a variety of anti-inflammatory nutrients. The tangy and zesty dressing made with lemon juice, Dijon mustard, and garlic adds flavor and makes this salad satisfying. Serve it with a slice of whole-grain bread for a complete and balanced meal. Enjoy!

LENTIL AND VEGETABLE SOUP

🌿 15 minutes ⏱ 45 minutes 🍴 6

Ingredients

- 1 cup dried green or brown lentils
- 1 tablespoon olive oil
- 1 onion, chopped
- 2 carrots, chopped
- 2 celery stalks, chopped
- 2 garlic cloves, minced
- 1 teaspoon ground cumin
- 1 teaspoon ground turmeric
- 1/2 teaspoon ground cinnamon
- 1/2 teaspoon ground ginger
- 6 cups low-sodium vegetable broth
- 1 (14.5-ounce) can of diced tomatoes, drained
- 2 cups chopped kale
- 1 tablespoon lemon juice
- Salt and pepper to taste (optional)

Preparation Steps

- In a large pot, heat the olive oil over medium heat. Add the onion, carrots, and celery and cook until softened, about 5 minutes.
- Add the garlic, cumin, turmeric, cinnamon, and ginger and cook for 1 minute until fragrant.
- Add the lentils, vegetable broth, and diced tomatoes to the pot. Bring to a boil, then reduce the heat to low and simmer for 30-40 minutes or until the lentils are tender.
- Stir in the chopped kale and lemon juice and continue cooking for 5-10 minutes until the kale has wilted.
- Season with salt and pepper to taste.
- Serve hot in bowls.

Calories: 178kcal | Carbohydrates: 27g | Protein: 10g | Fat: 4g | Saturated Fat: 1g | Sodium: 468mg | Fiber: 9g | Sugar: 5g

This lentil and vegetable soup is a nutritious and delicious option for an anti inflammatory lunch. Lentils are a great source of protein, fiber, and complex carbohydrates, while vegetables like kale, carrots, and celery provide an array of vitamins, minerals, and antioxidants. The spices used in this recipe, such as turmeric and ginger, are also known for their anti-inflammatory properties. This soup is a filling and nourishing meal that can help support a healthy immune system and reduce inflammation.

MEDITERRANEAN QUINOA SALAD

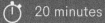 10 minutes 20 minutes 🍽 4

Ingredients

- 1 cup quinoa
- 2 cups water
- 1/4 cup diced red onion
- 1/4 cup diced red bell pepper
- 1/4 cup diced cucumber
- 1/4 cup chopped fresh parsley
- 1/4 cup chopped fresh mint

- 1/4 cup chopped kalamata olives
- 1/4 cup crumbled feta cheese
- 2 tablespoons extra-virgin olive oil
- 2 tablespoons fresh lemon juice
- 1/2 teaspoon ground cumin
- Salt and pepper to taste (optional)

Preparation Steps

- Rinse the quinoa in a fine mesh strainer and place in a medium saucepan with 2 cups of water. Bring to a boil, then reduce heat to low and simmer for 15-20 minutes or until the quinoa is tender and the water has been absorbed
- Remove from heat and let cool.
- Combine the cooled quinoa with the red onion, red bell pepper, cucumber, parsley, mint, olives, and feta cheese in a large bowl.
- Whisk the olive oil, lemon juice, cumin, salt, and pepper in a small bowl.
- Pour the dressing over the salad and toss to combine.
- Serve immediately, or chill in the refrigerator for up to 2 days.

Calories: 262kcal | Carbohydrates: 28g | Protein: 7g | Fat: 14g | Saturated Fat: 3g | Cholesterol: 8mg | Sodium: 279mg | Fiber: 4g | Sugar: 2g

This Mediterranean Quinoa Salad contains anti-inflammatory ingredients like quinoa, olive oil, lemon juice, and fresh herbs. Quinoa is an excellent plant-based protein and fiber source, while olive oil and lemon juice provide healthy fats and antioxidants. Fresh herbs like parsley and mint add flavor and anti-inflammatory compounds, while the kalamata olives and feta cheese add a salty and tangy taste. Enjoy this colorful and delicious salad as a side dish or a light meal!

ROASTED CHICKEN AND VEGETABLE BOWL

15 minutes   10 minutes   4

Ingredients

- 1 lb boneless, skinless chicken breasts
- 4 cups mixed vegetables (such as broccoli, bell peppers, zucchini, and carrots)
- 2 tablespoons olive oil
- 1 teaspoon dried rosemary
- 1 teaspoon dried thyme
- 1/2 teaspoon garlic powder
- Salt and pepper to taste (optional)

Preparation Steps

- Preheat the oven to 400°F (200°C) and line a baking sheet with parchment paper.
- Cut the chicken breasts into small cubes and place them in a bowl.
- Cut the mixed vegetables into small pieces and add them to the same bowl.
- Drizzle the olive oil over the chicken and vegetables and toss to coat.
- Sprinkle the rosemary, thyme, garlic powder, salt, and pepper over the mixture and toss again to coat.
- Spread the chicken and vegetables in a single layer on the prepared baking sheet.
- Roast in the oven for 20-25 minutes until the chicken is cooked and the vegetables are tender and golden brown.
- Serve immediately in bowls.

Calories: 265kcal | Carbohydrates: 10g | Protein: 27g | Fat: 13g | Saturated Fat: 2g | Cholesterol: 73mg | Sodium: 121mg | Fiber: 3g | Sugar: 4g

This Roasted Chicken and Vegetable Bowl is a protein-packed, nutrient-dense, anti-inflammatory meal. The chicken provides high-quality protein, while the mixed vegetables add fiber, vitamins, and minerals. Olive oil is a healthy fat with anti-inflammatory properties, while the herbs like rosemary and thyme add flavor and antioxidants. This recipe can easily be customized using different vegetables or herbs or adding whole grains like quinoa or brown rice. Enjoy this delicious and healthy bowl for a satisfying meal!

SARDINE AND ARUGULA SANDWICH

5 minutes | 0 minutes | 1

Ingredients

- 2 slices of whole-grain bread
- 1 can of sardines in water, drained
- 1/4 cup of arugula
- 1 tablespoon of chopped fresh basil
- 1 tablespoon of chopped fresh parsley
- 1/2 tablespoon of lemon juice
- 1/2 tablespoon of olive oil
- Salt and pepper to taste (optional)

Preparation Steps

- Toast the bread slices until golden brown and set aside.
- In a small bowl, mash the drained sardines with a fork.
- Add the arugula, chopped basil, parsley, lemon juice, olive oil, salt, and pepper to the bowl and mix well.
- Spread the sardine mixture onto one slice of toasted bread and top with the other slice.
- Serve immediately.

Calories: 281kcal | Carbohydrates: 23g | Protein: 18g | Fat: 14g | Saturated Fat: 2g | Cholesterol: 84mg | Sodium: 444mg | Fiber: 5g | Sugar: 2g

This Sardine and Arugula Sandwich is a delicious and omega-3-rich meal that's also anti-inflammatory. Sardines are a great source of omega-3 fatty acids, which have anti-inflammatory properties and are essential for brain and heart health. Arugula is a leafy green rich in vitamins and minerals, while the herbs like basil and parsley add flavor and antioxidants. Olive oil is a healthy fat with anti-inflammatory properties, while lemon juice adds a bright and tangy flavor. This recipe can easily be customized by using different types of bread or adding more vegetables like sliced tomatoes or cucumber. Enjoy this healthy and flavorful sandwich!

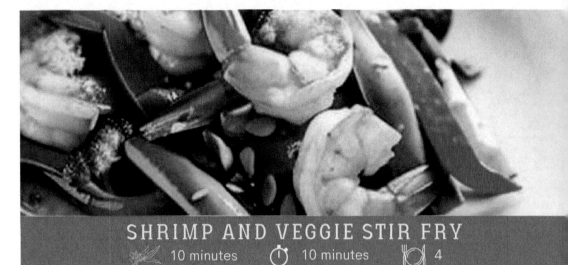

SHRIMP AND VEGGIE STIR FRY

10 minutes · 10 minutes · 4

Ingredients

- 1 pound of medium shrimp, peeled and deveined
- 2 cups of chopped mixed vegetables
- 2 cloves of garlic, minced
- 1 tablespoon of grated fresh ginger
- 1 tablespoon of olive oil
- 1 tablespoon of low-sodium soy sauce
- 1 tablespoon of rice vinegar
- 1/2 teaspoon of honey
- Salt and pepper to taste (optional)
- Optional garnish: sliced green onions and sesame seeds

Preparation Steps

- Whisk together the soy sauce, rice vinegar, honey, and a pinch of salt and pepper in a small bowl.
- Heat the olive oil in a large non-stick skillet over medium-high heat.
- Add the chopped vegetables, minced garlic, and grated ginger to the skillet and stir-fry for 3-4 minutes until the vegetables are crisp-tender.
- Add the shrimp to the skillet and stir-fry for 2-3 minutes until the shrimp are pink and cooked through.
- Pour the soy sauce mixture over the shrimp and vegetables and stir to combine.
- Cook for 1-2 minutes until the sauce thickens and coats the shrimp and vegetables.
- If desired, serve the stir-fry immediately, garnished with sliced green onions and sesame seeds.

Calories: 160kcal | Carbohydrates: 7g | Protein: 21g | Fat: 5g | Saturated Fat: 1g | Cholesterol: 191mg | Sodium: 482mg | Fiber: 2g | Sugar: 4g

This Shrimp and Veggie Stir Fry is a quick and easy anti-inflammatory meal. Shrimp is a lean protein with antioxidants, while mixed vegetables add fiber, vitamins, and minerals. Ginger and garlic are anti-inflammatory spices that add flavor and health benefits, while the soy sauce and rice vinegar provide a tangy and umami taste. This recipe can easily be customized by using different types of vegetables or adding more spices like red pepper flakes or sesame oil. Enjoy this healthy and delicious stir fry!

SPINACH AND MUSHROOM FRITTATA

10 minutes 25 minutes 4

Ingredients

- 6 large eggs
- 1/4 cup of milk
- 1 tablespoon of olive oil
- 1 small onion, chopped
- 2 cups of sliced mushrooms
- 2 cups of fresh spinach leaves
- 1 teaspoon of dried thyme
- 1 teaspoon of dried sage
- Salt and pepper to taste (optional)

Preparation Steps

- Preheat the oven to 375°F (190°C).
- Whisk together the eggs, milk, thyme, sage, salt, and pepper in a medium bowl.
- Heat the olive oil in a large oven-safe skillet over medium heat.
- Add the onion and sauté for 2-3 minutes or until softened.
- Add the mushrooms and continue to cook for 5-7 minutes, or until they have released their moisture and begin to brown.
- Add the spinach to the skillet and cook until wilted, about 2-3 minutes.
- Pour the egg mixture into the skillet, evenly distributing the vegetables.
- Cook the frittata over medium heat for 5-7 minutes or until the edges start to set.
- Transfer the skillet to the preheated oven and bake for 10-15 minutes until the frittata is set and golden.
- Remove from the oven and let the frittata cool for a few minutes before slicing and serving.

> Calories: 175kcal | Carbohydrates: 4g | Protein: 12g | Fat: 13g | Saturated Fat: 4g | Cholesterol: 281mg | Sodium: 177mg | Fiber: 1g | Sugar: 2g

This vegetarian frittata is packed with protein and healthy vegetables. The spinach and mushrooms provide a variety of vitamins and minerals, while the herbs used in the recipe have anti-inflammatory properties. Serve with a side salad or whole grain toast for a complete meal. Enjoy!

SWEET POTATO AND BLACK BEAN SALAD
15 minutes   25 minutes   4

Ingredients

- 2 sweet potatoes, peeled and cubed
- 1 can of black beans, drained and rinsed
- 1 red bell pepper, chopped
- 1/2 red onion, chopped
- 1/4 cup fresh cilantro, chopped
- 2 tablespoons olive oil
- 2 tablespoons fresh lime juice
- 1/2 teaspoon ground cumin
- 1/2 teaspoon chili powder
- Salt and pepper to taste (optional)

Preparation Steps

- Preheat the oven to 400°F (200°C).
- Spread the sweet potatoes in a single layer on a baking sheet, drizzle with 1 tablespoon of olive oil, and sprinkle with salt and pepper. Roast in the oven for 20-25 minutes or until tender and slightly caramelized.
- Combine the roasted sweet potatoes, black beans, red bell pepper, red onion, and cilantro in a large bowl.
- Whisk together the remaining 1 tablespoon of olive oil, lime juice, cumin, chili powder, salt, and pepper in a small bowl to make the dressing.
- Pour the dressing over the salad and toss to coat.
- Serve chilled or at room temperature.

Calories: 252kcal | Carbohydrates: 39g | Protein: 7g | Fat: 8g | Saturated Fat: 1g | Sodium: 156mg | Fiber: 10g | Sugar: 7g

This salad contains fiber, vitamins, and minerals from sweet potatoes, black beans, and anti-inflammatory spices like cumin and chili powder. It can be enjoyed as a side dish or a main meal and is perfect for meal prep or picnics.

TUNA AND AVOCADO SALAD
10 minutes   0 minutes   2

Ingredients

- 1 can of tuna in water, drained
- 1 ripe avocado, diced
- 1/4 cup of diced red onion
- 1/4 cup of chopped fresh parsley
- 2 tablespoons of olive oil
- 1 tablespoon of lemon juice
- Salt and pepper to taste (optional)

Preparation Steps

- Add the drained tuna, diced avocado, red onion, and chopped parsley in a medium bowl.
- In a small bowl, whisk together the olive oil and lemon juice.
- Pour the dressing over the tuna and avocado mixture and toss gently to coat.
- Season with salt and pepper to taste.
- Serve the salad immediately or store it in the refrigerator until ready.

Calories: 290kcal | Carbohydrates: 9g | Protein: 17g | Fat: 21g | Saturated Fat: 3g | Cholesterol: 24mg | Sodium: 260mg | Fiber: 6g | Sugar: 1g

This salad is an excellent source of protein and healthy fats from the tuna and avocado, and it also contains anti-inflammatory ingredients like red onion and parsley. It's quick and easy to prepare, making it an excellent option for a healthy lunch or dinner.

QUINOA AND ROASTED VEGETABLE SALAD

10 minutes   0 minutes   2

Ingredients

- 1/2 cup uncooked quinoa, rinsed
- 1 red bell pepper, sliced
- 1 zucchini, sliced
- 1 small red onion, sliced
- 1 tablespoon olive oil
- 1 teaspoon smoked paprika
- Salt and pepper to taste
- 2 cups baby spinach leaves
- 1/4 cup crumbled feta cheese
- 1/4 cup chopped fresh parsley
- 2 tablespoons lemon juice

Preparation Steps

- Preheat the oven to 400°F.
- Toss the red bell pepper, zucchini, and red onion with olive oil, smoked paprika, salt, and pepper in a large bowl.
- Spread the vegetables in a single layer on a baking sheet and roast in the oven for 20 minutes or until tender and lightly browned.
- Meanwhile, cook the quinoa according to the package instructions.
- Combine the cooked quinoa, roasted vegetables, baby spinach leaves, crumbled feta cheese, chopped parsley, and lemon juice in a large bowl.
- Toss well to combine and serve.

Calories: 310kcal | Carbohydrates: 34g | Protein: 10g | Fat: 16g | Saturated Fat: 4g | Cholesterol: 17mg | Sodium: 299mg | Fiber: 7g | Sugar: 6g

This salad is a perfect mix of nutritious ingredients that are anti-inflammatory including quinoa, which is rich in protein and fiber, and the roasted vegetables which are rich in antioxidants. The addition of feta cheese and spinach adds healthy fats and additional nutrients to the dish.

CHAPTER 8
DINNER

BAKED SALMON WITH BROCCOLI AND CAULIFLOWER

10 minutes   25 minutes   4

Ingredients

- 4 (4-6 oz) salmon fillets
- 1 small head of broccoli, chopped into florets
- 1 small head of cauliflower, chopped into florets
- 2 tbsp of olive oil
- 1 tsp of dried thyme
- 1 tsp of dried rosemary
- 1 tsp of garlic powder
- Salt and pepper to taste (optional)

Preparation Steps

- Preheat the oven to 400°F (200°C).
- Line a baking sheet with parchment paper.
- Mix the chopped broccoli, cauliflower, olive oil, dried thyme, rosemary, garlic powder, salt, and pepper in a large bowl.
- Spread the mixture out evenly on the prepared baking sheet.
- Place the salmon fillets on top of the vegetables, skin-side down.
- Season the salmon fillets with salt and pepper.
- Bake in the preheated oven for 20-25 minutes or until the salmon is cooked through and the vegetables are tender.
- Serve hot, and enjoy!

Calories: 297kcal | Carbohydrates: 9g | Protein: 30g | Fat: 17g | Saturated Fat: 3g | Sodium: 124mg | Fiber: 4g | Sugar: 3g

This Baked Salmon with Broccoli and Cauliflower recipe is a simple yet delicious and nutritious meal rich in omega-3 fatty acids and anti-inflammatory nutrients. The salmon fillets are baked to perfection and served on top of antioxidant-rich cruciferous vegetables, such as broccoli and cauliflower, seasoned with anti-inflammatory herbs like thyme and rosemary. This dish is perfect for a quick and healthy dinner that will satisfy your taste buds and support your overall health and well-being. Enjoy!

CHICKPEA AND VEGETABLE CURRY

10 minutes   25 minutes   4

Ingredients

- 1 tbsp olive oil
- 1 onion, chopped
- 3 cloves garlic, minced
- 1 tbsp grated ginger
- 1 tbsp ground cumin
- 1 tbsp ground turmeric
- 1 tsp paprika
- 1/2 tsp ground cinnamon
- 1/2 tsp ground coriander
- 1/4 tsp cayenne pepper
- 1 can (15 oz) chickpeas, drained and rinsed
- 2 cups chopped mixed vegetables 1 can (14.5 oz) diced tomatoes
- 1 cup vegetable broth
- 1/2 cup full-fat coconut milk
- Salt and pepper to taste (optional)
- Fresh cilantro for garnish

Preparation Steps

- Heat the olive oil in a large skillet over medium heat. Add the onion and cook until softened, about 5 minutes.
- Add the garlic, ginger, cumin, turmeric, paprika, cinnamon, coriander, and cayenne pepper. Cook, constantly stirring, for 1-2 minutes, until fragrant.
- Add the chickpeas, mixed vegetables, diced tomatoes, and vegetable broth. Bring to a simmer and cook for 15-20 minutes, until the vegetables are tender.
- Stir in the coconut milk and cook for 5 minutes until heated.
- Season with salt and pepper to taste.
- Garnish with fresh cilantro and serve over brown rice or quinoa.

Calories: 272kcal | Carbohydrates: 31g | Protein: 10g | Fat: 13g | Saturated Fat: 6g | Sodium: 599mg | Fiber: 10g | Sugar: 8g

This Chickpea and Vegetable Curry is a delicious and nourishing plant-based meal with anti-inflammatory ingredients. Chickpeas are a great source of plant-based protein and fiber, while mixed vegetables offer a variety of vitamins and minerals. The blend of spices used in the curry, including turmeric and cumin, have anti-inflammatory properties and add a depth of flavor to the dish. Serve this curry with brown rice or quinoa for a complete and satisfying meal.

GRILLED CHICKEN WITH ZUCCHINI AND SWEET POTATO

15 minutes   20 minutes   4

Ingredients

- 4 boneless, skinless chicken breasts
- 1/4 cup olive oil
- 1/4 cup fresh lemon juice
- 2 cloves garlic, minced
- 1 tsp dried oregano
- 1 tsp dried basil
- Salt and pepper, to taste (optional)

- 2 medium zucchinis, sliced
- 2 medium sweet potatoes, peeled and cut into 1-inch cubes
- 2 tbsp olive oil
- 1 tsp smoked paprika
- 1 tsp garlic powder
- Salt and pepper, to taste (optional)

Preparation Steps

- Preheat the grill to medium-high heat.
- Add olive oil, lemon juice, garlic, oregano, basil, salt, and pepper in a small bowl to make the chicken marinade.
- Place the chicken breasts in a resealable plastic bag and pour the marinade over them. Seal the bag and massage the chicken to ensure it is coated in the marinade. Refrigerate for at least 30 minutes.
- Toss the sliced zucchini and cubed sweet potatoes with olive oil, smoked paprika, garlic powder, salt, and pepper in a large bowl.
- Grill the chicken for 6-8 minutes per side or until the internal temperature reaches 165°F.
- While the chicken is cooking, grill the zucchini and sweet potatoes for 8-10 minutes or until tender and lightly charred.
- Serve the grilled chicken with the grilled zucchini and sweet potatoes on the side.

Calories: 406 kcal | Carbohydrates: 21g | Protein: 35g | Fat: 20g | Saturated Fat: 3g | Cholesterol: 96mg | Sodium: 242mg | Fiber: 4g | Sugar: 6g

This Grilled Chicken with Zucchini and Sweet Potato is a delicious and healthy meal perfect for a summer dinner. The chicken is marinated in a flavorful blend of olive oil, lemon juice, and herbs, while the zucchini and sweet potatoes are tossed in a spicy and smoky seasoning mix. All the ingredients are rich in anti-inflammatory nutrients, making this meal an excellent choice for those looking to reduce inflammation. Enjoy!

LENTIL AND VEGETABLE STEW RECIPE
15 minutes   35 minutes   6

Ingredients

- 1 cup of dried lentils, rinsed
- 2 cups of vegetable broth
- 1 onion, chopped
- 3 garlic cloves, minced
- 2 carrots, peeled and chopped
- 2 celery stalks, chopped
- 1 red bell pepper, chopped
- 1 zucchini, chopped

- 1 tablespoon of olive oil
- 1 teaspoon of ground cumin
- 1 teaspoon of paprika
- 1/2 teaspoon of ground turmeric
- 1/4 teaspoon of cayenne pepper
- 1 bay leaf
- Salt and black pepper to taste
- Chopped fresh parsley for garnish

Preparation Steps

- Heat olive oil in a large pot or Dutch oven over medium heat.
- Add the chopped onion, garlic, and sauté for 2-3 minutes until softened.
- Add chopped carrots, celery, red bell pepper, and zucchini, and stir well to combine.
- Add ground cumin, paprika, turmeric, cayenne pepper, and bay leaf, and stir well to coat the vegetables.
- Add the rinsed lentils and vegetable broth to the pot.
- Bring the mixture to a boil and then reduce the heat to low.
- Simmer the lentil stew for about 25-30 minutes or until the lentils are tender and the vegetables are cooked.
- Season with salt and black pepper to taste.
- Remove the bay leaf and discard it.
- Garnish the stew with chopped fresh parsley.
- Serve the lentil and vegetable stew hot with crusty bread or rice.

Calories: 174kcal | Carbohydrates: 28g | Protein: 11g | Fat: 2g | Saturated Fat: 1g | Sodium: 308mg | Fiber: 12g | Sugar: 6g

This Lentil and Vegetable Stew is a hearty and nutritious meal perfect for a cozy dinner on a chilly night. The lentils provide a great source of plant-based protein, fiber, and anti-inflammatory nutrients, while the vegetables offer a variety of vitamins and minerals. Combining herbs and spices like cumin, turmeric, and paprika adds flavor to the stew and offers anti-inflammatory benefits. Serve it with crusty bread or rice for a complete and satisfying meal. Enjoy!

QUINOA AND VEGETABLE STIR FRY RECIPE

10 minutes   20 minutes   4

Ingredients

- 1 cup quinoa
- 2 cups water or vegetable broth
- 1 tablespoon olive oil
- 1 tablespoon minced garlic
- 1 tablespoon minced ginger
- 1 red bell pepper, sliced
- 1 yellow bell pepper, sliced
- 1 cup broccoli florets
- 1 cup sliced carrots
- 1/2 cup sliced scallions
- 1 tablespoon of soy sauce
- 1 tablespoon rice vinegar
- 1 teaspoon toasted sesame oil
- Salt and pepper to taste (optional)

Preparation Steps

- Rinse the quinoa and drain well.
- Bring the water or vegetable broth to a boil in a medium pot. Add the quinoa, cover, and reduce heat to low. Simmer for 15-20 minutes or until the liquid has been absorbed and the quinoa is tender.
- Heat the olive oil over medium-high heat in a large skillet or wok. Add the garlic and ginger and stir fry for 1-2 minutes or until fragrant.
- Add the bell peppers, broccoli, and carrots to the skillet and stir fry for 5-7 minutes or until the vegetables are tender but still crisp.
- Add the cooked quinoa and scallions to the skillet and stir fry for 1-2 minutes to heat through.
- Whisk the tamari sauce, rice vinegar, toasted sesame oil, salt, and pepper in a small bowl.
- Pour the sauce over the stir fry and stir well to coat the vegetables and quinoa.
- Serve hot, and enjoy!

Calories: 234kcal | Carbohydrates: 37g | Protein: 7g | Fat: 8g | Saturated Fat: 1g | Sodium: 317mg | Fiber: 6g | Sugar: 6g

This quinoa and vegetable stir fry is a nutritious and delicious meal that can be ready in 30 minutes. Quinoa provides a plant-based source of protein, and fresh vegetables offer an array of anti-inflammatory nutrients like vitamin C and fiber. Combining ginger and garlic adds a delicious flavor to the dish and provides anti-inflammatory benefits. Tamari sauce, rice vinegar, and toasted sesame oil create a savory and umami-rich sauce that ties everything together. Serve this dish as a standalone meal or alongside some grilled chicken or tofu for extra protein. Enjoy!

ROASTED TURKEY WITH BRUSSELS SPROUTS AND BUTTERNUT SQUASH

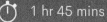 15 minutes 1 hr 45 mins 🍴 8

Ingredients

- 1 (12-14 pound) turkey, giblets removed
- 1 large butternut squash, peeled and cubed
- 1 pound Brussels sprouts, trimmed and halved
- 4 cloves garlic, minced
- 1 onion, chopped
- 1 tablespoon fresh rosemary
- 1 tablespoon fresh thyme, chopped
- 2 tablespoons olive oil
- Salt and pepper to taste (optional)

Preparation Steps

- Preheat the oven to 350°F (175°C).
- Rinse the turkey and pat it dry with paper towels. Season the turkey inside and out with salt and pepper.
- Toss the butternut squash, Brussels sprouts, onion, garlic, rosemary, thyme, olive oil, salt, and pepper in a large bowl.
- Place the turkey in a large roasting pan and arrange the vegetable mixture around it.
- Roast the turkey for 1 hour and then baste it with pan juices. Continue roasting the turkey for 45 minutes to 1 hour until a meat thermometer inserted into the thickest part of the thigh reaches 165°F (74°C).
- Transfer the turkey to a serving platter and let it rest for 10-15 minutes before carving.
- Serve the turkey with the roasted vegetables on the side.

Calories: 468kcal | Carbohydrates: 20g | Protein: 55g | Fat: 18g | Saturated Fat: 4g | Cholesterol: 167mg | Sodium: 187mg | Fiber: 5g | Sugar: 5g

This Roasted Turkey with Brussels Sprouts and Butternut Squash is a delicious and nutritious meal for holiday dinners or any special occasion. The turkey provides a healthy source of protein, while the butternut squash and Brussels sprouts offer a variety of anti-inflammatory nutrients. The herbs and spices add flavor and depth to the dish, making it a crowd-pleaser. Plus, it's easy to prepare and can be customized to your taste preferences. Enjoy!

GRILLED SHRIMP AND VEGETABLE SKEWERS

20 minutes   10 minutes   2

Ingredients

- 1 pound large shrimp, peeled and deveined
- 1 red bell pepper, cut into 1-inch pieces
- 1 yellow bell pepper, cut into 1-inch pieces
- 1 zucchini, sliced into 1/4-inch rounds
- 1 red onion, cut into 1-inch pieces
- 1/4 cup olive oil
- 2 cloves garlic, minced
- 1 tablespoon fresh thyme, chopped
- 1/2 teaspoon sea salt
- 1/4 teaspoon black pepper
- 4 skewers

Preparation Steps

- Preheat the grill to medium-high heat.
- Mix olive oil, garlic, thyme, salt, and black pepper in a large bowl.
- Add the shrimp, bell peppers, onion, and zucchini to the bowl, and toss until the vegetables and shrimp are well coated.
- Thread the shrimp and vegetables onto skewers, alternating between the shrimp and vegetables.
- Place the skewers on the preheated grill and cook for 2-3 minutes on each side until the shrimp is pink and cooked through.
- Serve the skewers immediately.

Calories: 255kcal | Carbohydrates: 11g | Protein: 22g | Fat: 14g | Saturated Fat: 2g | Cholesterol: 214mg | Sodium: 534mg | Fiber: 3g | Sugar: 5g

These Grilled Shrimp and Vegetable Skewers are a perfect dinner option for those following an anti-inflammatory diet. Shrimp is an excellent source of omega-3 fatty acids known for their anti-inflammatory properties. The bell peppers and zucchini are also rich in anti-inflammatory nutrients, making this dish delicious and healthy. The thyme and garlic add a delightful depth of flavor, making this dish a crowd-pleaser. Plus, it's easy to prepare and can be customized to your taste preferences. Enjoy!

SPAGHETTI SQUASH WITH MEAT SAUCE

10 minutes   1 hour   4

Ingredients

- 1 spaghetti squash, halved and seeded
- 1 pound lean ground beef
- 1 onion, chopped
- 2 cloves garlic, minced
- 1 can (14.5 ounces) diced tomatoes
- 1 can (8 ounces) tomato sauce
- 1 tablespoon dried basil
- 1 teaspoon dried oregano
- 1/2 teaspoon sea salt
- 1/4 teaspoon black pepper
- 2 tablespoons olive oil

Preparation Steps

- Preheat oven to 375°F (190°C).
- Place the spaghetti squash halves, cut side down, on a baking sheet, and bake for 45-50 minutes or until the squash is tender and easily pierced with a fork.
- In a large skillet, heat olive oil over medium-high heat. Add ground beef and cook until browned, stirring occasionally.
- Add the onion and garlic to the skillet and cook for 2-3 minutes or until the onion is tender.
- Add the diced tomatoes, tomato sauce, basil, oregano, sea salt, and black pepper to the skillet. Bring the mixture to a boil, then reduce heat to low and simmer for 10-15 minutes.
- Use a fork to scrape the spaghetti squash into strands.
- Serve the spaghetti squash topped with the meat sauce.

Calories: 338kcal | Carbohydrates: 16g | Protein: 27g | Fat: 19g | Saturated Fat: 6g | Cholesterol: 81mg | Sodium: 838mg | Fiber: 4g | Sugar: 9g

This Spaghetti Squash with Meat Sauce recipe is a perfect dinner option for those following a low-carb and gluten-free diet. Spaghetti squash is a great low-carb substitute for pasta and is rich in anti-inflammatory nutrients. The meat sauce is flavorful and includes anti-inflammatory herbs like basil and oregano. The dish is easy to prepare and can be customized to your taste preferences. Plus, it's a healthy and delicious way to enjoy a classic Italian dish without gluten and excess carbs. Enjoy!

SWEET POTATO AND BLACK BEAN ENCHILADAS

🌿 20 minutes   ⏱ 30 minutes   🍽 4

Ingredients

- 1 sweet potato, peeled and diced
- 1 can (15 ounces) of black beans, drained and rinsed
- 1 small onion, chopped
- 2 cloves garlic, minced
- 1 teaspoon ground cumin
- 1 teaspoon chili powder
- 1/4 teaspoon smoked paprika
- 1/4 teaspoon sea salt
- 1/4 teaspoon black pepper
- 8 corn tortillas
- 1 can (10 ounces) enchilada sauce
- 1/2 cup shredded cheese
- 2 tablespoons chopped fresh cilantro

Preparation Steps

- Preheat oven to 375°F (190°C).
- In a large skillet, heat olive oil over medium-high heat. Add sweet potato and cook for 8-10 minutes until tender and lightly browned.
- Add black beans, onion, garlic, cumin, chili powder, smoked paprika, sea salt, and black pepper to the skillet. Cook for 2-3 minutes or until the onion is tender.
- Warm the corn tortillas in the microwave or griddle to make them pliable.
- Spoon the sweet potato and black bean mixture onto the center of each tortilla and roll tightly. Place the enchiladas seam-side down in a 9x13-inch baking dish.
- Pour the enchilada sauce over the enchiladas and sprinkle with shredded cheese.
- Bake for 20-25 minutes until the cheese is melted and bubbly.
- Garnish with chopped cilantro before serving.

Calories: 397kcal | Carbohydrates: 66g | Protein: 16g | Fat: 9g | Saturated Fat: 4g | Cholesterol: 18mg | Sodium: 1147mg | Fiber: 13g | Sugar: 6g

This Sweet Potato and Black Bean Enchiladas recipe is a satisfying and plant-based dinner option for those looking for a healthy and delicious meal. The sweet potato and black bean filling provides a good source of fiber and protein, while the anti-inflammatory spices like cumin and chili powder add flavor and depth to the dish. The recipe is easy to prepare and can be customized to your taste preferences. Plus, it's a great way to enjoy a classic Mexican dish in a healthy and nutritious way. Enjoy!

ZUCCHINI NOODLE PAD THAI

🌿 15 minutes ⏱ 10 minutes 🍴 2

Ingredients

- 2 tablespoons tamari
- 2 tablespoons lime juice
- 2 tablespoons honey
- 1 tablespoon rice vinegar
- 1 tablespoon fish sauce
- 1 tablespoon grated ginger
- 1 clove garlic, minced
- 1/4 teaspoon red pepper flakes

- 4 medium zucchinis, spiralized
- 1 red bell pepper, sliced
- 1 carrot, peeled and shredded
- 2 green onions, sliced
- 1/4 cup chopped peanuts
- 2 tablespoons chopped fresh cilantro

Preparation Steps

- Whisk together the tamari, lime juice, honey, rice vinegar, fish sauce, ginger, garlic, and red pepper flakes in a small bowl to make the sauce.
- Spiralize the zucchinis using a spiralizer or a julienne peeler.
- Heat a large skillet over medium-high heat. Add the bell pepper and carrot to the skillet and cook for 2-3 minutes or until slightly softened.
- Add the zucchini noodles to the skillet and cook for 1-2 minutes or until tender.
- Pour the sauce over the noodles and vegetables in the skillet and toss to coat.
- Top with green onions, chopped peanuts, and fresh cilantro.

Calories: 148kcal | Carbohydrates: 22g | Protein: 6g | Fat: 6g | Saturated Fat: 1g | Sodium: 576mg | Fiber: 3g | Sugar: 15g

This Zucchini Noodle Pad Thai recipe is a healthy and flavorful dinner option for those looking for a low-carb and gluten-free meal. The zucchini noodles are a great alternative to traditional wheat-based noodles and provide a good source of fiber and vitamins. The homemade pad Thai sauce has anti-inflammatory ingredients like lime juice and tamari, adding a tangy and savory flavor. The recipe is easy to prepare and can be customized to your taste preferences. Plus, it's a great way to enjoy a classic Thai dish in a healthy and nutritious way. Enjoy!

CHAPTER 9
FISH & SEA FOOD

BAKED HALIBUT WITH ASPARAGUS AND CHERRY TOMATOES

10 minutes   15 minutes   4

Ingredients

- 4 (6-ounce) halibut fillets
- 1 bunch of asparagus, trimmed
- 1 pint cherry tomatoes, halved
- 2 tablespoons olive oil
- 2 cloves garlic, minced
- 1 teaspoon dried thyme
- Salt and pepper to taste (optional)
- Lemon wedges for serving

Preparation Steps

- Preheat the oven to 400°F (200°C).
- Place the halibut fillets in a baking dish.
- Arrange the asparagus and cherry tomatoes around the halibut fillets.
- Whisk the olive oil, garlic, thyme, salt, and pepper in a small bowl.
- Drizzle the olive oil mixture over the halibut fillets, asparagus, and cherry tomatoes.
- Bake in the oven for 12-15 minutes until the halibut is cooked and the vegetables are tender.
- Serve hot with lemon wedges.

Calories: 265kcal | Carbohydrates: 8g | Protein: 35g | Fat: 10g | Saturated Fat: 2g | Cholesterol: 85mg | Sodium: 105mg | Fiber: 3g | Sugar: 4g

This Baked Halibut with Asparagus and Cherry Tomatoes recipe is a simple and nutritious dinner option for busy weeknights. The halibut provides a healthy source of protein, while the asparagus and cherry tomatoes offer a variety of vitamins and antioxidants. The garlic and thyme add flavor and depth to the dish, making it a flavorful and satisfying meal. The recipe is easy to prepare and can be customized to your taste preferences. Plus, it's a great way to enjoy a healthy and delicious seafood dish at home. Enjoy!

GRILLED SHRIMP AND PINEAPPLE SKEWERS

10 minutes   15 minutes   4

Ingredients

- 1 lb shrimp, peeled and deveined
- 1 medium pineapple, peeled, cored, and cut into chunks
- 1 red onion, cut into chunks
- 2 tablespoons olive oil
- 2 tablespoons honey
- 2 tablespoons fresh lime juice
- 1 tablespoon chili powder
- 1/2 teaspoon ground cumin
- Salt and pepper to taste (optional)
- 8 wooden skewers, soaked in water for 30 minutes

Preparation Steps

- Preheat the grill to medium-high heat.
- Whisk together the olive oil, honey, lime juice, chili powder, cumin, salt, and pepper in a small bowl to make the marinade.
- Thread the shrimp, pineapple, and onion onto the skewers, alternating between each ingredient.
- Brush the skewers with the marinade, making sure to coat all sides.
- Place the skewers on the grill and cook on each side for 3-4 minutes until the shrimp are pink and opaque, and the pineapple is lightly charred.
- Remove the skewers from the grill and let them rest for a few minutes before serving.

Calories: 236kcal | Carbohydrates: 29g | Protein: 21g | Fat: 5g | Saturated Fat: 1g | Cholesterol: 191mg | Sodium: 434mg | Fiber: 3g | Sugar: 23g

This Grilled Shrimp and Pineapple Skewers recipe is a delicious tropical dinner option for warm summer nights. The shrimp provides a healthy source of protein, while the pineapple offers a variety of vitamins and anti-inflammatory properties. The honey and lime marinade adds a sweet and tangy flavor to the dish, making it a crowd-pleaser. The recipe is easy to prepare and can be customized to your taste preferences. Plus, it's a great way to enjoy a healthy and delicious grilled seafood dish at home. Enjoy!

SALMON AND AVOCADO SALAD RECIPE

15 minutes   10 minutes   2

Ingredients

- 2 salmon fillets (6 oz each), skin removed
- 4 cups mixed greens
- 1 ripe avocado, diced
- 1/2 red onion, thinly sliced
- 1/4 cup chopped fresh cilantro
- 1/4 cup chopped fresh parsley
- 1 tablespoon olive oil

- Salt and pepper, to taste (optional)
- 1/2 cucumber, diced
- 2 tablespoons extra-virgin olive oil
- 1 tablespoon apple cider vinegar
- 1 tablespoon honey
- 1 tablespoon Dijon mustard
- 1 garlic clove, minced
- Salt and pepper, to taste (optional)

Preparation Steps

- Preheat the oven to 400°F (200°C). Line a baking sheet with parchment paper.
- Season the salmon fillets with salt and pepper, and place them on the prepared baking sheet. Drizzle with 1 tablespoon of olive oil. Bake for 10-12 minutes or until cooked through.
- In a small bowl, whisk together the dressing ingredients. Set aside.
- Combine the mixed greens, avocado, red onion, cucumber, cilantro, and parsley in a large bowl.
- When the salmon is done, remove it from the oven and let it cool for a few minutes.
- Divide the salad between two plates. Top each dish with a salmon fillet.
- Drizzle the dressing over the salad and serve immediately.

Calories: 503kcal | Carbohydrates: 23g | Protein: 36g | Fat: 31g | Saturated Fat: 5g | Cholesterol: 78mg | Sodium: 145mg | Fiber: 9g | Sugar: 10g

This Salmon and Avocado Salad perfectly combines protein, healthy fats, and fiber-rich greens. Salmon is rich in omega-3 fatty acids, which have anti-inflammatory properties, while avocado is packed with monounsaturated fats, fiber, and antioxidants. The salad dressing adds a tangy and sweet flavor that complements the dish perfectly. This salad is easy to prepare, nutritious, and satisfying, making it an ideal meal for any day of the week.

SEARED SCALLOPS WITH BROCCOLI AND CARROTS RECIPE

10 minutes   15 minutes   2

Ingredients

- 10-12 large sea scallops
- 1 tablespoon olive oil
- 1/2 teaspoon smoked paprika
- Salt and pepper, to taste
- For the Broccoli and Carrots:
- 2 cups broccoli florets
- 1 cup sliced carrots

- 1 tablespoon olive oil
- 1 teaspoon dried oregano
- 1/4 cup olive oil
- 2 cloves garlic, minced
- 2 tablespoons fresh lemon juice
- 1/2 teaspoon lemon zest
- 1/2 teaspoon dried basil
- Salt and pepper, to taste (optional)

Preparation Steps

- Preheat a skillet over medium-high heat.
- Pat the scallops dry and season them with smoked paprika, salt, and pepper.
- Add 1 tablespoon of olive oil to the skillet, then place the scallops in the skillet and cook for 2-3 minutes per side, until browned and cooked through. Remove from skillet and set aside.
- Heat 1 tablespoon of olive oil over medium-high heat in a separate skillet. Add the broccoli and carrots and cook for 5-7 minutes, until slightly tender—season with dried oregano, salt, and pepper.
- To make the Lemon Garlic Sauce, whisk together the olive oil, garlic, lemon juice, lemon zest, dried basil, salt, and pepper in a small bowl.
- Serve the seared scallops alongside the broccoli and carrots, drizzled with the Lemon Garlic Sauce.

Calories: 280kcal | Carbohydrates: 16g | Protein: 20g | Fat: 16g | Saturated Fat: 2g | Cholesterol: 37mg | Sodium: 294mg | Fiber: 5g | Sugar: 5g

This Seared Scallops with Broccoli and Carrots recipe is not only delicious but it's also packed with anti-inflammatory ingredients. The scallops are a great source of protein, omega-3 fatty acids, and vitamin B12, which can help reduce inflammation. Broccoli and carrots are high in fiber, vitamins, and minerals which can also help reduce inflammation. The Lemon Garlic Sauce adds flavor and provides additional anti-inflammatory benefits from the garlic and lemon. This dish is easy to prepare, nutrient-dense, and perfect for a nutritious gourmet dinner.

TUNA STEAK WITH ROASTED BRUSSELS SPROUTS RECIPE

 10 minutes 20 minutes ❘○❘ 2

Ingredients

- 2 tuna steaks (6 oz each)
- 1 tablespoon olive oil
- 1/2 teaspoon paprika
- Salt and pepper, to taste
- 2 cups Brussels sprouts, halved
- 1/2 teaspoon garlic powder

- 1/4 cup plain Greek yogurt
- 1 tablespoon lemon juice
- 1 tablespoon olive oil
- 1 tablespoon chopped fresh dill
- 1/2 teaspoon garlic powder
- Salt and pepper, to taste (optional)

Preparation Steps

- Preheat the oven to 400°F (200°C).
- Pat the tuna steaks dry with a paper towel and season them with paprika, salt, and pepper.
- Heat 1 tablespoon of olive oil in a skillet over medium-high heat. Add the tuna steaks and cook for 3-4 minutes per side until browned on the outside and slightly pink in the middle.
- Remove from skillet and set aside.
- Toss the Brussels sprouts in 1 tablespoon of olive oil, garlic powder, salt, and pepper. Place them on a baking sheet and roast for 15-20 minutes until golden brown and crispy.
- Mix the Greek yogurt, lemon juice, chopped dill, garlic powder, salt, and pepper in a small bowl to make the Lemon Dill Sauce.
- Serve the tuna steaks with the roasted Brussels sprouts and drizzle with the Lemon Dill Sauce.

Calories: 295kcal | Carbohydrates: 12g | Protein: 33g | Fat: 13g | Saturated Fat: 2g | Cholesterol: 46mg | Sodium: 121mg | Fiber: 4g | Sugar: 3g

This Tuna Steak with Roasted Brussels Sprouts recipe is a flavorful, nutrient-dense dinner option perfect for an anti-inflammatory diet. Tuna is an excellent source of protein, omega-3 fatty acids, and vitamin D, which can help reduce inflammation. Brussels sprouts are also packed with anti-inflammatory nutrients, including fiber, vitamin C, and antioxidants. The Lemon Dill Sauce adds a tangy and refreshing flavor to the dish and provides additional anti-inflammatory benefits from the lemon and dill. This recipe is easy to prepare, satisfying, and perfect for a healthy and delicious dinner.

COD WITH GREEN BEANS AND TOMATOES RECIPE

10 minutes   20 minutes   2

Ingredients

- 2 cod fillets (6 oz each)
- 1 tablespoon olive oil
- 1/2 teaspoon garlic powder
- Salt and pepper, to taste (optional)
- 2 cups green beans, trimmed
- 1 cup cherry tomatoes, halved
- 1 tablespoon olive oil
- 1 garlic clove, minced

Preparation Steps

- Preheat the oven to 400°F (200°C).
- Place the cod fillets on a baking sheet and season them with garlic powder, salt, and pepper. Drizzle with 1 tablespoon of olive oil.
- Toss the green beans and cherry tomatoes in a bowl with 1 tablespoon of olive oil, minced garlic, salt, and pepper.
- Spread the green bean mixture around the cod fillets on the baking sheet.
- Bake for 15-20 minutes, until the cod is cooked and the vegetables are tender.
- Serve the cod with the green beans and tomatoes on the side.

Calories: 238kcal | Carbohydrates: 12g | Protein: 28g | Fat: 9g | Saturated Fat: 1g | Cholesterol: 56mg | Sodium: 77mg | Fiber: 4g | Sugar: 6g

This Cod with Green Beans and Tomatoes recipe is a simple and nutritious dinner option perfect for any night of the week. Cod is a lean protein source rich in omega-3 fatty acids with anti-inflammatory properties. Green beans and tomatoes contain antioxidants, vitamins, and minerals that help reduce inflammation. This dish is easy to prepare, low in calories, and satisfying, making it an ideal meal for anyone following an anti-inflammatory diet.

GRILLED SWORDFISH WITH MANGO SALSA RECIPE

15 minutes   10 minutes   2

Ingredients

- 2 swordfish steaks (6 oz each)
- 1 tablespoon olive oil
- 1 teaspoon paprika
- 1/2 teaspoon garlic powder
- Salt and pepper, to taste

- 1 mango, peeled and diced
- 1/4 red onion, diced
- 1/4 cup diced red bell pepper
- 1/4 cup chopped fresh cilantro
- 1 tablespoon lime juice
- 1 tablespoon olive oil

Preparation Steps

- Preheat the grill to medium-high heat.
- Season the swordfish steaks with olive oil, paprika, garlic powder, salt, and pepper.
- Grill the swordfish steaks for 4-5 minutes per side or until cooked through.
- While the swordfish is grilling, prepare the mango salsa by combining the diced mango, red onion, red bell pepper, cilantro, lime juice, olive oil, salt, and pepper in a bowl.
- Serve the grilled swordfish steaks with mango salsa on top.

Calories: 342kcal | Carbohydrates: 17g | Protein: 35g | Fat: 16g | Saturated Fat: 2g | Cholesterol: 99mg | Sodium: 95mg | Fiber: 3g | Sugar: 12g

This Grilled Swordfish with Mango Salsa recipe is a flavorful and nutritious dinner option for summertime. Swordfish is an excellent source of protein and omega-3 fatty acids with anti-inflammatory properties. The mango salsa adds a sweet and tangy flavor and contains antioxidants, vitamins, and minerals that help reduce inflammation. This dish is easy to prepare and makes for a satisfying and healthy meal.

LOBSTER TAIL WITH ASPARAGUS AND LEMON RECIPE

 15 minutes 10 minutes 🍽 2

Ingredients

- 2 lobster tails
- 1 lb asparagus, trimmed
- 1 lemon, sliced
- 2 tablespoons olive oil
- Salt and pepper, to taste(optional)

Preparation Steps

- Preheat the oven to 400°F (200°C).
- Using kitchen scissors, cut through the top shell of the lobster tail and remove the meat, leaving the meat attached to the bottom of the shell.
- Season the lobster tail with salt, pepper, and 1 tablespoon olive oil. Place the lemon slices on top of the lobster meat.
- Wrap each lobster tail with aluminum foil and place them on a baking sheet. Bake for 15-20 minutes until the lobster meat is cooked through.
- While the lobster is cooking, heat the remaining 1 tablespoon of olive oil in a pan over medium-high heat. Add the asparagus and season with salt and pepper. Cook for 5-7 minutes until the asparagus is tender and slightly browned.
- Serve the lobster tail with the roasted lemon slices on top and the asparagus on the side.

Calories: 211kcal | Carbohydrates: 7g | Protein: 27g | Fat: 9g | Saturated Fat: 1g | Cholesterol: 85mg | Sodium: 455mg | Fiber: 3g | Sugar: 3g

This Lobster Tail with Asparagus and Lemon recipe is a luxurious, low-carb dinner option for a special occasion. Lobster is an excellent source of protein and contains healthy fats, while asparagus is an antioxidant-rich vegetable high in fiber and low in calories. The lemon adds a bright and refreshing flavor to the dish and provides vitamin C, which helps support a healthy immune system. This dish is easy to prepare and makes for a delicious and healthy meal.

MISO GLAZED SALMON WITH BOK CHOY RECIPE

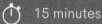 10 minutes 15 minutes 🍽 2

Ingredients

- 2 salmon fillets (6 oz each)
- 2 tablespoons white miso paste
- 1 tablespoon rice vinegar
- 1 tablespoon sesame oil
- 1 tablespoon soy sauce
- 1 garlic clove, minced
- 4 baby bok choy, halved
- 1 tablespoon honey
- 1 tablespoon olive oil
- 1 garlic clove, minced
- Salt and pepper, to taste (optional)

Preparation Steps

- Preheat the oven to 425°F (218°C).
- Whisk together the miso paste, honey, rice vinegar, sesame oil, soy sauce, and minced garlic in a small bowl to make the miso glaze.
- Season the salmon fillets with salt and pepper, then brush the miso glaze generously over the top of each fillet.
- Place the salmon fillets on a baking sheet lined with parchment paper and bake for 12-15 minutes or until the salmon is cooked.
- While the salmon is cooking, heat the olive oil in a large skillet over medium-high heat. Add the garlic and cook for 1 minute.
- Add the bok choy to the skillet and season with salt and pepper. Cook for 3-5 minutes or until the bok choy is tender and slightly charred.
- Serve the miso glazed salmon with the bok choy on the side.

Calories: 410kcal | Carbohydrates: 18g | Protein: 35g | Fat: 22g | Saturated Fat: 4g | Cholesterol: 78mg | Sodium: 1262mg | Fiber: 3g | Sugar: 11g

This Miso Glazed Salmon with Bok Choy recipe is a savory and satisfying dinner option packed with protein, healthy fats, and nutrient-dense vegetables. The miso glaze provides a delicious umami flavor and also contains probiotics that can help support gut health. Bok choy is a low-calorie vegetable that's high in vitamins A and C, as well as other antioxidants. This dish is easy to prepare and makes for a flavorful and healthy meal.

SHRIMP AND VEGETABLE STIR FRY WITH QUINOA RECIPE

15 minutes 15 minutes 2

Ingredients

- 1 cup quinoa, rinsed and drained
- 2 cups water
- 1 tablespoon olive oil
- 1/2 pound raw shrimp, deveined
- 1 red bell pepper, sliced
- 1 yellow bell pepper, sliced
- 1 zucchini, sliced
- 1 yellow squash, sliced
- 1 cup snow peas
- 1/2 onion, sliced

- 3 garlic cloves, minced
- 1 tablespoon fresh ginger, grated
- 1/4 cup low-sodium soy sauce
- 2 tablespoons rice vinegar
- 1 tablespoon honey
- 1 tablespoon cornstarch
- 2 tablespoons water
- Salt and pepper to taste (optional)
- Chopped green onions and sesame seeds for garnish

Preparation Steps

- Combine the quinoa, 2 cups of water, and a pinch of salt in a medium saucepan. Bring to a boil, reduce heat to low, cover, and simmer until tender and the water has been absorbed about 15-20 minutes.
- While the quinoa cooks heat the olive oil in a large skillet over medium-high heat. Add the shrimp and cook until pink, about 2-3 minutes per side. Remove from skillet and set aside.
- Add sliced peppers, zucchini, squash, snow peas, onion, garlic, and ginger to the same skillet. Cook until the vegetables are tender-crisp, about 5-7 minutes.
- Whisk together the soy sauce, rice vinegar, honey, cornstarch, and water in a small bowl.
- Pour the mixture over the vegetables and stir to coat. Cook until the sauce has thickened, about 2-3 minutes.
- Return the shrimp to the skillet and toss it with the vegetables and sauce.
- Serve the stir-fry over a bed of cooked quinoa. Garnish with chopped green onions and sesame seeds.

Calories: 310 kcal | Carbohydrates: 41g | Protein: 22g | Fat: 6g | Saturated Fat: 1g | Cholesterol: 95mg | Sodium: 662mg | Fiber: 6g | Sugar: 10g

This Shrimp and Vegetable Stir Fry with Quinoa is a delicious and healthy meal that is quick and easy to make. Shrimp is an excellent source of lean protein, while colorful vegetables provide fiber, vitamins, and minerals. Quinoa is a nutritious and gluten-free grain that adds texture and flavor to the dish. The soy sauce and rice vinegar add savory and tangy flavors, while the honey provides a touch of sweetness. This dish is perfect for busy weeknights when you want a healthy and satisfying meal.

CHAPTER 10
POULTRY

GRILLED CHICKEN WITH RAINBOW VEGETABLES

🌿 20 minutes ⏱ 20 minutes 🍽 4

Ingredients

For the Chicken:
- 4 boneless, skinless chicken breasts
- 2 tablespoons olive oil
- 2 garlic cloves, minced
- 1 teaspoon dried oregano
- 1 teaspoon dried basil
- 1/2 teaspoon salt
- 1/4 teaspoon black pepper

For the Vegetables:
- 2 cups cherry tomatoes, halved
- 1 red bell pepper, chopped
- 1 yellow bell pepper, chopped
- 1 green bell pepper, chopped
- 1 small red onion, chopped
- 2 tablespoons olive oil
- 1/2 teaspoon salt
- 1/4 teaspoon black pepper

Preparation Steps

- Preheat the grill to medium-high heat.
- Mix olive oil, garlic, oregano, basil, salt, and black pepper in a small bowl.
- Brush the chicken breasts with the olive oil mixture.
- Mix the cherry tomatoes, bell peppers, and red onion in a large bowl. Toss with 2 tablespoons of olive oil and season with salt and black pepper.
- Grill the chicken for 6-7 minutes per side or until the internal temperature reaches 165°F (74°C). Remove from the grill and let rest for 5 minutes.
- While the chicken is resting, grill the vegetables in a grilling basket for 8-10 minutes or until they are tender and slightly charred.
- Serve the chicken with the grilled vegetables on the side.

Calories: 349kcal | Carbohydrates: 11g | Protein: 34g | Fat: 19g | Saturated Fat: 3g | Cholesterol: 96mg | Sodium: 673mg | Fiber: 3g | Sugar: 6g

This Grilled Chicken with Rainbow Vegetables is a delicious and nutritious meal perfect for a summertime dinner. The chicken is marinated with flavorful herbs and grilled to perfection, while the vegetables are grilled until tender and slightly charred. This dish is high in protein and fiber and low in carbs, making it an excellent option for those watching their carbohydrate intake. Plus, the combination of colorful vegetables provides a wide range of vitamins, minerals, and antioxidants. Serve this dish with a side of whole-grain bread or a small portion of brown rice for a complete and balanced meal.

LEMON HERB CHICKEN WITH SWEET POTATOES

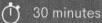 15 minutes 30 minutes 🍽 4

Ingredients

For the Lemon Herb Chicken:
- 4 boneless, skinless chicken breasts
- 2 tablespoons olive oil
- 1/4 cup fresh lemon juice
- 2 teaspoons lemon zest
- 2 cloves garlic, minced
- 1 tablespoon chopped fresh parsley
- 1 tablespoon chopped fresh thyme

- 1/2 teaspoon salt
- 1/4 teaspoon black pepper

For the Roasted Sweet Potatoes:
- 2 sweet potatoes, peeled and cubed
- 2 tablespoons olive oil
- 1/2 teaspoon garlic powder
- 1/2 teaspoon paprika
- 1/2 teaspoon salt
- 1/4 teaspoon black pepper

Preparation Steps

- Preheat the oven to 400°F (200°C).
- Whisk together olive oil, lemon juice, lemon zest, garlic, parsley, thyme, salt, and pepper in a small bowl. Place chicken breasts in a shallow dish and pour the marinade over them.
- Marinate in the refrigerator for at least 15 minutes or up to 4 hours.
- Toss sweet potato cubes with olive oil, garlic powder, paprika, salt, and pepper. Spread them out in a single layer on a baking sheet.
- Roast the sweet potatoes for 25-30 minutes until tender and lightly browned.
- While the sweet potatoes are roasting, preheat the grill to medium-high heat. Grill the chicken for 6-7 minutes per side or until the internal temperature reaches 165°F (74°C).
- Serve the grilled chicken with the roasted sweet potatoes on the side.

> Calories: 331kcal | Carbohydrates: 20g | Protein: 29g | Fat: 15g | Saturated Fat: 2g | Cholesterol: 72mg | Sodium: 480mg | Fiber: 4g | Sugar: 6g

This Lemon Herb Chicken with Roasted Sweet Potatoes recipe is a delicious and easy-to-make meal with flavor and nutrition. The lemon herb marinade gives the chicken a tangy and refreshing taste, while the roasted sweet potatoes add a touch of sweetness and a healthy dose of fiber. This dish is also a great source of protein, vitamins, and minerals, making it a well-rounded meal that will keep you satisfied and energized.

ROASTED CHICKEN WITH BRUSSELS SPROUTS

10 minutes   0 minutes   2

Ingredients

For the Chicken:
- 4 chicken thighs, bone-in, and skin-on
- 2 tbsp olive oil
- 2 tbsp lemon juice
- 1 tbsp honey
- 1 tbsp turmeric powder
- 1 tsp garlic powder
- 1 tsp ground ginger
- Salt and pepper to taste (optional)

For the Brussels Sprouts:
- 1 lb Brussels sprouts, halved
- 2 tbsp olive oil
- 1 tsp garlic powder
- Salt and pepper to taste (optional)

Preparation Steps

- Preheat the oven to 400°F (200°C).
- Whisk together the olive oil, lemon juice, honey, turmeric powder, garlic powder, ground ginger, salt, and pepper in a small bowl.
- Arrange the chicken thighs in a baking dish, skin side up. Pour the turmeric mixture over the chicken, making sure it is well-coated.
- Arrange the halved Brussels sprouts around the chicken in the baking dish. Drizzle them with olive oil, and sprinkle with garlic powder, salt, and pepper.
- Roast in the oven for 35-40 minutes until the chicken is cooked and the Brussels sprouts are tender and caramelized.
- Serve hot, and enjoy!

Calories: 420kcal | Carbohydrates: 14g | Protein: 27g | Fat: 29g | Saturated Fat: 7g | Cholesterol: 141mg | Sodium: 141mg | Fiber: 5g | Sugar: 6g

This Turmeric Roasted Chicken with Brussels Sprouts recipe is an anti-inflammatory dinner option. Turmeric contains curcumin, which has potent anti-inflammatory properties and is an excellent addition to chicken marinade. Brussels sprouts are high in fiber and antioxidants; roasting them brings out their natural sweetness. The chicken thighs are a good source of protein, and the skin-on option provides healthy fats to the dish. This recipe is easy to make and perfect for a weeknight dinner.

CHICKEN AND VEGETABLE SKEWERS WITH SAUCE

25 minutes   10 minutes   4

Ingredients

For the Skewers:

- 1 lb boneless, skinless chicken breasts cut into 1-inch pieces
- 1 red bell pepper, cut into 1-inch P
- 1 yellow bell pepper, cut into 1-inch P
- 1 red onion, cut into 1-inch pieces
- 1 zucchini, sliced into rounds
- 8 wooden skewers, soaked in water

For the Tahini Sauce:

- 1/4 cup tahini paste
- 1/4 cup water
- 3 tablespoons freshly squeezed lemon juice
- 1 garlic clove, minced
- 1/4 teaspoon salt
- 1/4 teaspoon ground cumin

Preparation Steps

- Preheat the grill to medium-high heat.
- Thread chicken, bell peppers, onion, and zucchini onto skewers, alternating between each ingredient.
- Whisk together tahini paste, water, lemon juice, garlic, salt, and cumin in a small bowl to make the tahini sauce.
- Place skewers on the grill and cook for 8-10 minutes, occasionally turning, until chicken is cooked through and vegetables are lightly charred.
- Serve skewers with tahini sauce on the side.

Calories: 253kcal | Carbohydrates: 10g | Protein: 29g | Fat: 12g | Saturated Fat: 2g | Cholesterol: 73mg | Sodium: 226mg | Fiber: 2g | Sugar: 4g

This Chicken and Vegetable Skewers with Tahini Sauce recipe perfectly balances protein and fiber-rich vegetables. The chicken is an excellent source of lean protein, while the bell peppers and zucchini boost vitamin C and antioxidants. The tahini sauce provides a tangy and nutty flavor that complements the dish perfectly. The recipe is easy to prepare and great for a quick, healthy weeknight dinner.

ROSEMARY CHICKEN THIGHS WITH SQUASH

10 minutes   40 minutes   4

Ingredients

For the Chicken:
- 4 chicken thighs, bone-in, and skin-on
- 1 tbsp chopped fresh rosemary
- 2 cloves garlic, minced
- 1 tbsp olive oil
- Salt and pepper to taste (optional)

For the Butternut Squash:
- 1 medium butternut squash, peeled and cut into 1-inch cubes
- 1 tbsp olive oil
- 1 tsp ground cinnamon
- 1/2 tsp ground nutmeg
- Salt and pepper to taste (optional)

Preparation Steps

- Preheat the oven to 400°F (200°C).
- Mix the rosemary, garlic, olive oil, salt, and pepper in a small bowl.
- Rub the chicken thighs with the rosemary mixture, and coat them evenly.
- Place the chicken thighs in a baking dish for 30-35 minutes or until the internal temperature reaches 165°F (75°C).
- While the chicken is cooking, prepare the butternut squash.
- Toss the butternut squash cubes with olive oil, cinnamon, nutmeg, salt, and pepper in a separate bowl.
- Spread the seasoned butternut squash cubes in a single layer on a baking sheet and roast in the oven for 20-25 minutes or until they are tender and golden brown.
- Once the chicken and butternut squash is done, remove them from the oven and serve hot.

Calories: 393kcal | Carbohydrates: 15g | Protein: 24g | Fat: 27g | Saturated Fat: 6g | Cholesterol: 141mg | Sodium: 89mg | Fiber: 3g | Sugar: 3g

This Rosemary Garlic Chicken Thighs with Butternut Squash recipe is a delicious comforting dinner option packed with nutrients. The chicken thighs provide protein and essential amino acids, while the butternut squash offers a range of vitamins, minerals, and fiber. The rosemary and garlic in the chicken thighs add flavor and anti-inflammatory properties. The cinnamon and nutmeg in the butternut squash add a warm, comforting taste and have anti-inflammatory and antioxidant properties. This dish is easy to prepare and perfect for a cozy night.

CHICKEN AND BROCCOLI STIR FRY WITH RICE

10 minutes   20 minutes   4

Ingredients

For the stir fry:
- 1 pound boneless, skinless chicken breast cut into bite-sized pieces
- 1 head broccoli, cut into florets
- 1 red bell pepper, sliced
- 1 yellow onion, sliced
- 2 cloves garlic, minced
- 2 tablespoons avocado oil
- Salt and pepper, to taste (optional)

For the sauce:
- 1/4 cup low-sodium soy sauce
- 1 tablespoon honey
- 1 tablespoon cornstarch
- 1 teaspoon ground ginger
- 1/2 teaspoon garlic powder
- 1/4 teaspoon red pepper flakes

For the brown rice:
- 1 cup brown rice
- 2 cups water
- Pinch of salt

Preparation Steps

- Rinse brown rice in cold water and drain. Place rice, water, and a pinch of salt in a pot and boil. Reduce heat, cover, and let simmer for 40-45 minutes until fully cooked.
- In a small bowl, whisk together the sauce ingredients and set aside.
- In a large skillet or wok, heat avocado oil over medium-high heat. Add chicken and stir-fry until browned and cooked, about 5-7 minutes.
- Add broccoli, red bell pepper, onion, and garlic to the skillet and stir-fry for 5-7 minutes or until the vegetables are tender.
- Pour the sauce over the chicken and vegetables, and stir to coat evenly. Cook for 1-2 minutes or until the sauce has thickened.
- Serve the stir-fry with brown rice.

Calories: 410kcal | Carbohydrates: 51g | Protein: 32g | Fat: 9g | Saturated Fat: 1g | Cholesterol: 73mg | Sodium: 683mg | Fiber: 5g | Sugar: 8g

This chicken and broccoli stir-fry with brown rice is quick, easy, healthy, and delicious. It is packed with lean protein from chicken, fiber-rich vegetables, and whole-grain brown rice. The sauce perfectly balances sweet and savory flavors while keeping the dish low in sodium. This meal can be customized with different vegetables or protein sources to suit personal preferences, making it a versatile and convenient option for any day of the week.

CHICKEN AND ZUCCHINI NOODLE SOUP

10 minutes   25 minutes   4

Ingredients

- 1 tablespoon olive oil
- 1 onion, chopped
- 2 garlic cloves, minced
- 1 lb chicken breast, cubed
- 6 cups chicken broth
- 2 medium zucchinis, spiralized into noodles
- 1 teaspoon dried thyme
- 1 teaspoon dried oregano
- Salt and pepper, to taste (optional)
- Fresh parsley, chopped, for garnish

Preparation Steps

- Heat olive oil in a large pot over medium heat. Add onion and garlic and cook until softened, about 3-4 minutes.
- Add chicken breast and cook until browned on all sides, about 5-7 minutes.
- Pour in chicken broth, thyme, oregano, salt, and pepper. Bring to a boil, then reduce heat and let simmer for 10-15 minutes.
- Add zucchini noodles and cook for 5 minutes or until tender.
- Serve hot, garnished with fresh parsley.

Calories: 217 kcal | Carbohydrates: 7g | Protein: 31g | Fat: 7g | Saturated Fat: 1g | Cholesterol: 73mg | Sodium: 1031mg | Fiber: 2g | Sugar: 3g

This chicken and zucchini noodle soup is a delicious and nutritious way to enjoy a comforting bowl of soup. Zucchini noodles make a great low-carb alternative to traditional noodles, while the chicken provides protein and the broth offers nourishing benefits. The herbs and spices add flavor and anti-inflammatory properties to the soup, making it an excellent option for anyone looking for a healthy and satisfying meal. Enjoy this soup on a chilly day or whenever you need a comforting bowl of soup.

TURKEY BURGERS WITH PORTOBELLO BUNS

15 minutes   15 minutes   4

Ingredients

- 1 pound ground turkey
- 1/2 cup grated zucchini
- 1/2 cup grated carrot
- 1 teaspoon smoked paprika
- 1/2 teaspoon salt
- 1/4 teaspoon black pepper
- 4 large portobello mushroom caps
- 2 tablespoons olive oil
- Toppings: sliced avocado, tomato, lettuce

Preparation Steps

- Preheat the grill or grill pan to medium-high heat.
- Mix the ground turkey, grated zucchini, grated carrot, smoked paprika, salt, and pepper in a large bowl. Form the mixture into 4 patties.
- Brush the portobello mushroom caps with olive oil on both sides, and sprinkle with salt and pepper.
- Grill the turkey burgers on each side for 6-8 minutes or until fully cooked. Grill the portobello mushroom caps on each side for 3-4 minutes or until tender.
- Assemble the burgers by placing a portobello mushroom cap with the gill side on a plate. Place a turkey burger on top of the portobello mushroom cap and add desired toppings such as avocado, tomato, and lettuce.
- Serve immediately.

Calories: 275kcal | Carbohydrates: 8g | Protein: 28g | Fat: 15g | Saturated Fat: 2g | Cholesterol: 62mg | Sodium: 431mg | Fiber: 3g | Sugar: 3g

These grilled turkey burgers with portobello buns are a delicious and healthy dinner option that is perfect for those who follow a low-carb or gluten-free diet. The combination of ground turkey, grated zucchini, and grated carrot provides protein and vegetables, while the portobello mushroom buns add a rich and meaty flavor. The toppings of avocado, tomato, and lettuce add more nutrients and flavor to the dish. This recipe is easy to customize with different toppings to suit your personal preferences.

MOROCCAN CHICKEN WITH QUINOA PILAF RECIPE

10 minutes   0 minutes   2

Ingredients

For the chicken:
- 1 pound boneless, skinless chicken breasts cut into bite-sized pieces
- 1 tablespoon olive oil
- 1 tablespoon Moroccan spice blend
- 1/2 teaspoon salt

For the quinoa pilaf:
- 1 cup quinoa

- 2 cups low-sodium chicken broth
- 1 tablespoon olive oil
- 1/4 cup chopped onion
- 1/4 cup chopped carrot
- 1/4 cup chopped celery
- 1 teaspoon ground cumin
- 1/2 teaspoon paprika
- 1/4 teaspoon salt
- 1/4 teaspoon black pepper

Preparation Steps

- Combine chicken, olive oil, Moroccan spice blend, and salt in a large bowl. Toss until the chicken is well-coated.
- Preheat a grill or grill pan to medium-high heat. Grill chicken for 6-8 minutes per side or until cooked through.
- Meanwhile, rinse the quinoa in cold water and drain. In a medium saucepan, heat olive oil over medium heat. Add onion, carrot, celery, and sauté for 3-4 minutes or until the vegetables are slightly softened.
- Add cumin, paprika, salt, black pepper, quinoa, and chicken broth to the saucepan, and boil. Reduce heat, cover, and let simmer for 15-20 minutes until the liquid is fully absorbed and the quinoa is tender.
- Serve the grilled Moroccan chicken with the quinoa pilaf.

Calories: 381kcal | Carbohydrates: 34g | Protein: 35g | Fat: 11g | Saturated Fat: 2g | Cholesterol: 73mg | Sodium: 605mg | Fiber: 5g | Sugar: 3g

This Moroccan chicken with quinoa pilaf is a delicious and nutritious meal perfect for dinner. The Moroccan spice blend adds a warm and exotic flavor to the chicken, while the quinoa pilaf is packed with fiber and nutrients. This meal can be customized with different vegetables or protein sources to suit personal preferences, making it a versatile and convenient option for any day of the week.

PESTO CHICKEN WITH ROASTED VEGETABLES

 10 minutes   0 minutes   ⭐ 2

Ingredients

For the chicken:

- 4 boneless, skinless chicken breasts
- 1/2 cup basil pesto
- 1 tablespoon olive oil
- Salt and pepper, to taste

For the vegetables:

- 2 medium zucchini, sliced
- 2 bell peppers, sliced
- 1 large red onion, sliced
- 2 cloves garlic, minced
- 1 tablespoon olive oil
- Salt and pepper, to taste (optional)

Preparation Steps

- Preheat oven to 425°F (220°C).
- In a small bowl, mix the basil pesto and olive oil.
- Place the chicken breasts in a large resealable plastic bag and pour the pesto mixture over them. Seal the bag and shake to coat the chicken evenly.
- Place the marinated chicken on a baking sheet lined with parchment paper—season with salt and pepper to taste.
- Toss the sliced zucchini, bell peppers, red onion, and minced garlic with olive oil in a separate bowl—season with salt and pepper to taste.
- Add the seasoned vegetables to the baking sheet with the chicken.
- Roast in the oven for 25-30 minutes or until the chicken is cooked and the vegetables are tender and slightly charred.
- Serve the chicken and roasted vegetables hot with quinoa, rice, or your preferred grain.

Calories: 350kcal | Carbohydrates: 12g | Protein: 34g | Fat: 19g | Saturated Fat: 3g | Cholesterol: 94mg | Sodium: 372mg | Fiber: 3g | Sugar: 6g

This pesto chicken with roasted vegetables is a simple and delicious dinner that is easy to prepare and packed with flavor. The basil pesto adds a rich and savory taste to the chicken, while the roasted vegetables provide a sweet and slightly charred flavor that perfectly complements the dish. This meal is also anti-inflammatory and nutrient-dense, with various colorful vegetables that provide vitamins and minerals and a protein-rich chicken that keeps you full and satisfied. Serve with quinoa pilaf or your preferred grain for a complete and satisfying meal.

CHAPTER 11
SNACKS

AVOCADO AND TOMATO SALSA WITH WHOLE GRAIN CHIPS

🌿 10 minutes   ⏱ 0 minutes   🍴 4

Ingredients

For the salsa:
- 2 ripe avocados, diced
- 2 medium tomatoes, diced
- 1/4 red onion, finely chopped
- 1 jalapeno pepper, seeded and finely chopped
- 1/4 cup fresh cilantro, chopped
- Juice of 1 lime
- Salt and pepper, to taste (optional)

For the chips:
- 4 whole grain tortillas
- 2 tablespoons olive oil
- Salt, to taste (optional)

Preparation Steps

- Preheat the oven to 375°F (190°C).
- For the chips: Brush each tortilla with olive oil and sprinkle with salt. Cut into triangles and place on a baking sheet. Bake for 10-12 minutes or until crispy and lightly browned.
- For the salsa: In a medium bowl, combine the diced avocados, tomatoes, red onion, jalapeno pepper, and cilantro. Squeeze lime juice over the mixture and season with salt and pepper to taste. Mix well.
- Serve the salsa with whole-grain chips on the side.

Calories: 240kcal | Carbohydrates: 26g | Protein: 5g | Fat: 15g | Saturated Fat: 2g | Sodium: 203mg | Fiber: 8g | Sugar: 4g

This avocado and tomato salsa with whole grain chips is a tasty and nutritious snack perfect for any time of day. Combining avocado, tomato, and jalapeno pepper creates a refreshing and flavorful salsa with healthy fats and fiber. The whole-grain chips add crunch and texture while providing a good source of complex carbohydrates. This snack is easy to prepare and can be enjoyed as a quick and satisfying snack or an appetizer at parties and gatherings.

CARROT AND HUMMUS DIP WITH BELL PEPPER SLICES

10 minutes   0 minutes   4

Ingredients

- 2 large carrots, peeled and chopped
- 1/4 cup tahini
- 1/4 cup lemon juice
- 1/4 cup olive oil
- 2 garlic cloves, minced
- Salt and pepper, to taste (optional)
- 2 bell peppers, sliced

Preparation Steps

- In a food processor, blend the chopped carrots until they are finely chopped.
- Add the tahini, lemon juice, olive oil, minced garlic, salt, and pepper to the food processor with the carrots. Blend until the mixture is smooth and well combined.
- Taste the dip and adjust the seasoning if needed.
- Serve the carrot and hummus dip with sliced bell peppers for dipping.

Calories: 185 kcal | Carbohydrates: 12g | Protein: 3g | Fat: 15g | Saturated Fat: 2g | Sodium: 70mg | Fiber: 4g | Sugar: 5g

This carrot and hummus dip is a great way to add more vegetables—the combination of sweet carrots and savory hummus pairs well with the crunchy and slightly sweet bell peppers. The dip is packed with fiber and healthy fats from the tahini and olive oil, making it a filling and nutritious snack. Plus, it's easy to make and can be stored in the fridge for up to 3 days.

TURMERIC ROASTED CHICKPEAS

5 minutes   25 minutes   4

Ingredients

- 1 can (15 oz) chickpeas, drained and rinsed
- 1 tablespoon avocado oil
- 1 teaspoon turmeric
- 1/2 teaspoon paprika
- 1/2 teaspoon garlic powder
- 1/2 teaspoon sea salt

Preparation Steps

- Preheat the oven to 400°F.
- Combine chickpeas, avocado oil, turmeric, paprika, garlic powder, and sea salt in a bowl. Toss until the chickpeas are evenly coated.
- Spread the chickpeas in a single layer on a baking sheet lined with parchment paper.
- Bake for 25 minutes or until the chickpeas are crispy and golden brown.
- Serve as a snack or as a crunchy topping on a salad.

Calories: 145kcal | Carbohydrates: 18g | Protein: 6g | Fat: 5g | Saturated Fat: 1g | Sodium: 305mg | Fiber: 5g | Sugar: 3g

These turmeric-roasted chickpeas are a crunchy, satisfying snack packed with protein and anti-inflammatory benefits. Turmeric, paprika, and garlic powder add flavor and have anti-inflammatory properties. This snack is easy to make and can be customized by adding your favorite seasonings. They are great for munching on during the day or as a crunchy topping on a salad.

CHIA SEED PUDDING WITH BERRIES

🌿 5 minutes   ⏱ 2 hours   🍽 2

Ingredients

- 1/4 cup chia seeds
- 1 cup unsweetened almond milk (or any other milk of your choice)
- 1 tablespoon honey (optional)
- 1/2 teaspoon vanilla extract
- 1 cup mixed berries (such as blueberries, strawberries, and raspberries)
- Optional toppings: chopped nuts, coconut flakes, additional berries

Preparation Steps

- In a mixing bowl, whisk chia seeds, almond milk, honey (if using), and vanilla extract until well combined.
- Cover the bowl with plastic wrap and refrigerate for at least 2 hours, or overnight, until the chia seeds have absorbed the liquid and formed a pudding-like consistency.
- Once the chia seed pudding has been set, please stir it to ensure no clumps.
- To serve, divide the pudding into two bowls or glasses and top with mixed berries and any other desired toppings.
- Enjoy as a snack or a healthy breakfast option!

Calories: 190kcal | Carbohydrates: 24g | Protein: 6g | Fat: 9g | Saturated Fat: 1g | Sodium: 93mg | Fiber: 12g | Sugar: 9g

This chia seed pudding with berries is a perfect snack for those looking for something healthy and filling. Chia seeds are packed with fiber, protein, and omega-3 fatty acids, while berries contain antioxidants and anti-inflammatory properties. The almond milk used in this recipe provides a dairy-free alternative low in calories and nutrients. The sweetness of honey and the flavor of vanilla extract complement the nuttiness of chia seeds and the tartness of the berries. This pudding can be made and stored in the fridge for a quick snack or breakfast.

CUCUMBER ROLL-UPS WITH SMOKED SALMON

15 minutes   ⏱ 0 minutes   🍽 4

Ingredients

- 1 large cucumber
- 4 oz smoked salmon
- 1/4 cup whipped cream cheese
- 2 tbsp chopped fresh dill
- 1 tbsp capers (optional)
- Salt and pepper, to taste (optional)

Preparation Steps

- Thinly slice the cucumber lengthwise into strips using a mandoline or vegetable peeler.
- In a small bowl, mix the whipped cream cheese, chopped dill, and capers (if using) together until well combined.
- Lay the cucumber strips on a cutting board or flat surface. Spread a thin layer of the cream cheese mixture over each cucumber strip.
- Lay a small piece of smoked salmon over the cream cheese mixture on each cucumber strip.
- Season with salt and pepper to taste.
- Roll up the cucumber strips, starting from one end and rolling tightly until the end.
- Use a toothpick to secure each roll-up.
- Serve immediately or store in the refrigerator for up to 2 hours before serving.

Calories: 86 kcal | Carbohydrates: 2g | Protein: 5g | Fat: 6g | Saturated Fat: 2g | Cholesterol: 11mg | Sodium: 255mg | Fiber: 0g | Sugar: 1g

These cucumber roll-ups with smoked salmon are a delicious and nutritious snack perfect for an anti-inflammatory diet. Smoked salmon is high in omega-3 fatty acids, which have anti-inflammatory properties, while cucumber is a low-calorie, anti-inflammatory vegetable. Adding whipped cream cheese and fresh dill provides a creamy and tangy flavor to the roll-ups, while the capers (optional) add a touch of saltiness. This snack is high in protein and low in carbohydrates, making it an excellent option for those following a low-carb or keto diet.

BAKED SWEET POTATO CHIPS

 10 minutes 25 minutes 🍴 4

Ingredients

- 2 medium sweet potatoes
- 2 tbsp olive oil
- 1 tsp garlic powder
- 1 tsp paprika
- 1/2 tsp salt
- 1/4 tsp black pepper

Preparation Steps

- Preheat the oven to 375°F (190°C) and line a baking sheet with parchment paper.
- Thinly slice the sweet potatoes into rounds using a mandoline or sharp knife.
- Whisk together the olive oil, garlic powder, paprika, salt, and black pepper in a small bowl.
- Dip each sweet potato round into the olive oil mixture, coating both sides well.
- Place the sweet potato rounds in a single layer on the prepared baking sheet.
- Bake in the oven for 20-25 minutes or until the edges are browned, and the chips are crispy.
- Remove the chips from the oven and let them cool for a few minutes before serving.

Calories: 116 kcal | Carbohydrates: 16g | Protein: 1g | Fat: 6g | Saturated Fat: 1g | Sodium: 316mg | Fiber: 3g | Sugar: 4g

These baked sweet potato chips are a healthy, delicious snack perfect for an anti-inflammatory diet. Sweet potatoes are high in fiber, which can help to reduce inflammation in the body. The spices used in this recipe, such as garlic powder and paprika, also have anti-inflammatory properties. These chips are easy to make and are a great alternative to traditional potato chips. They are crispy, savory, and satisfying, making them an excellent daily snack.

ALMOND BUTTER AND APPLE SLICES

5 minutes   0 minutes   2

Ingredients

- 1 medium apple, cored and sliced
- 2 tbsp almond butter
- 1/2 tsp cinnamon

Preparation Steps

- Wash the apple and slice it into thin rounds.
- In a small bowl, stir the almond butter and cinnamon until well combined.
- Dip the apple slices into the almond butter mixture and spread it evenly.
- Arrange the apple slices on a plate and serve immediately.

Calories: 177 kcal | Carbohydrates: 20g | Protein: 4g | Fat: 11g | Saturated Fat: 1g | Sodium: 39mg | Fiber: 5g | Sugar: 13g

This almond butter and apple slices snack is a perfect example of a satisfying and nutrient-dense anti-inflammatory snack. Apples are a great source of fiber, while almond butter is high in healthy fats, protein, and vitamin E. The addition of cinnamon not only adds a delicious flavor but also provides additional anti-inflammatory benefits. This snack is quick and easy to prepare and can be enjoyed as a mid-day or post-workout snack to refuel your body.

ZUCCHINI FRITTERS WITH GREEK YOGURT DIP

15 minutes · 15 minutes · 2

Ingredients

For the fritters:
- 2 medium zucchini, grated
- 1/4 cup almond flour
- 1 egg
- 1/4 cup chopped fresh parsley
- 1 garlic clove, minced

- Salt and pepper, to taste
- 2 tbsp olive oil

For the dip:
- 1/2 cup plain Greek yogurt
- 1 tbsp lemon juice
- Salt and pepper, to taste

Preparation Steps

- Preheat the oven to 375°F (190°C) and line a baking sheet with parchment paper.
- Grate the zucchini into a large bowl and squeeze out excess moisture.
- Add almond flour, egg, parsley, garlic, salt, and pepper to the bowl and mix well.
- Heat olive oil in a large non-stick skillet over medium-high heat.
- Drop spoonfuls of zucchini mixture into the skillet, forming small fritters. Cook for 2-3 minutes on each side until golden brown.
- Transfer the fritters to the prepared baking sheet and bake in the oven for 5-7 minutes or until fully cooked.
- Mix yogurt, lemon juice, salt, and pepper in a small bowl until welfare the dip l combined.
- Serve zucchini fritters with Greek yogurt dip on the side.

Calories: 200 kcal | Carbohydrates: 12g | Protein: 7g | Fat: 15g | Saturated Fat: 2g | Sodium: 368mg | Fiber: 3g | Sugar: 4g

These zucchini fritters with Greek yogurt dip are a flavorful, fiber-rich snack perfect for an anti-inflammatory diet. Zucchini is an excellent source of fiber and antioxidants, while almond flour adds healthy fats and protein. Greek yogurt is high in protein and probiotics, which can help reduce gut inflammation. Combining fresh herbs and garlic adds a delicious flavor to these fritters, making them a satisfying snack or light meal.

KALE CHIPS WITH LEMON TAHINI DIP

🌿 10 minutes ⏱ 20 minutes 🍴 4

Ingredients

For the kale chips:
- 1 large bunch of kale, stems removed and torn into bite-sized pieces
- 1 tbsp olive oil
- 1/4 tsp salt

- 1/4 tsp black pepper

For the dip:
- 1/4 cup tahini
- 1/4 cup water
- 1 tbsp lemon juice
- 1 garlic clove, minced
- Salt and pepper, to taste (optional)

Preparation Steps

- **For the kale chips:** Preheat the oven to 350°F (175°C) and line a baking sheet with parchment paper.
- Massage the kale pieces with olive oil, salt, and pepper in a large bowl until the leaves are coated.
- Spread the kale pieces in a single layer on the prepared baking sheet.
- Bake in the preheated oven for 15-20 minutes or until the edges of the leaves are crispy and slightly browned.
- **For the dip:** Whisk together the tahini, water, lemon juice, garlic, salt, and pepper in a small bowl until smooth and well combined.
- Taste the dip and adjust the seasoning if needed.
- Serve the kale chips with the lemon tahini dip on the side.

Calories: 120 kcal | Carbohydrates: 8g | Protein: 4g | Fat: 9g | Saturated Fat: 1g | Sodium: 164mg | Fiber: 2g | Sugar: 1g

These kale chips with lemon tahini dip are a crunchy, nutrient-dense snack perfect for an anti-inflammatory diet. Kale is packed with vitamins, minerals, and antioxidants that can help to reduce inflammation in the body. The lemon tahini dip adds a zesty and creamy flavor that complements the crispy kale chips. Tahini is an excellent source of healthy fats and protein, while lemon juice adds a bright and refreshing taste. This snack is easy to make and can be enjoyed anytime for a satisfying and healthy snack.

COCONUT YOGURT PARFAIT WITH GRANOLA

🌿 10 minutes   ⏱ 0 minutes   🍽 2

Ingredients

- 1 cup mixed berries (such as strawberries, blueberries, and raspberries)
- 1 cup coconut yogurt
- 1/2 cup granola

Preparation Steps

- In two parfait glasses or bowls, layer 1/4 cup of coconut yogurt at the bottom of each glass.
- Top the yogurt with a layer of mixed berries, dividing them evenly between the two glasses.
- Add another 1/4 cup of coconut yogurt on top of the berries.
- Sprinkle 1/4 cup of granola over the yogurt in each glass.
- Finish by adding another layer of mixed berries on top of the granola.
- Serve and enjoy!

Calories: 308 kcal | Carbohydrates: 40g | Protein: 7g | Fat: 14g | Saturated Fat: 5g | Sodium: 99mg | Fiber: 7g | Sugar: 20g

This coconut yogurt parfait with berries and granola is a delicious and nutritious snack perfect for an anti-inflammatory diet. Coconut yogurt is an excellent alternative to dairy yogurt and is packed with healthy fats and probiotics that can support gut health and reduce inflammation. Berries are rich in antioxidants and fiber, while the granola adds a crunchy and satisfying texture. This snack is easy to make and can be enjoyed for breakfast, as a snack, or as a healthy dessert.

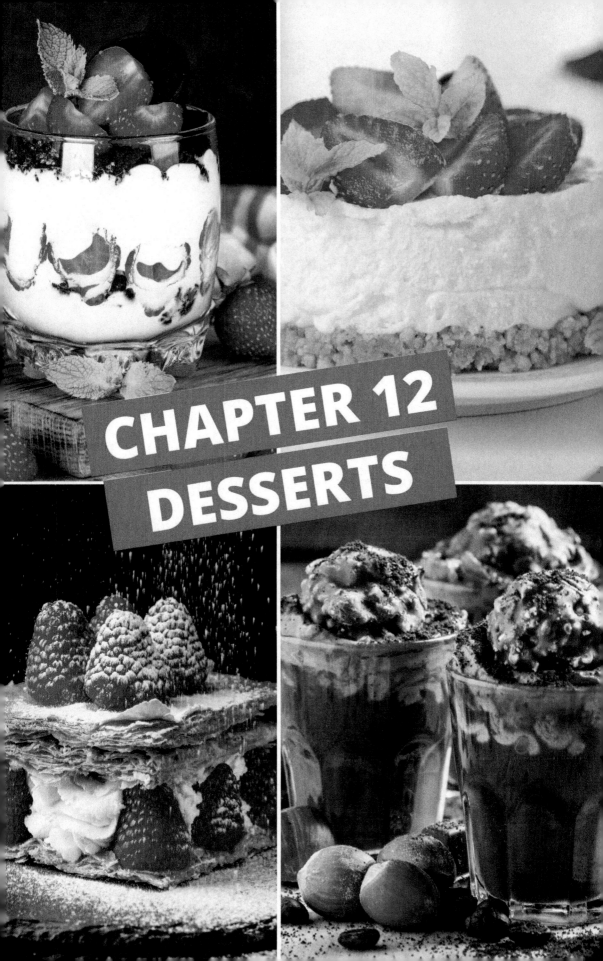

CHAPTER 12
DESSERTS

BLUEBERRY OATMEAL BARS

15 minutes　　35 minutes　　12

Ingredients

For the crust and topping:
- 1 1/2 cups rolled oats
- 1 cup whole wheat flour
- 1/2 cup coconut oil, melted
- 1/4 cup honey
- 1/4 tsp salt

- 1 tsp cinnamon

For the filling:
- 2 cups blueberries, fresh or frozen
- 1/4 cup honey
- 1 tbsp cornstarch
- 1 tbsp lemon juice

Preparation Steps

- Preheat the oven to 350°F (180°C). Grease an 8-inch square baking dish with coconut oil.
- Mix the oats, whole wheat flour, melted coconut oil, honey, salt, and cinnamon in a large bowl until well combined.
- Reserve 1 cup of the mixture for the topping and press the rest into the bottom of the prepared baking dish.
- Mix the blueberries, honey, cornstarch, and lemon juice separately until the berries are evenly coated.
- Spread the blueberry mixture over the crust in the baking dish.
- Crumble the reserved oat mixture on top of the blueberries.
- Bake for 35-40 minutes or until the top is golden brown.
- Let the bars cool completely in the pan before slicing and serving.

Calories: 221 kcal | Carbohydrates: 31g | Protein: 3g | Fat: 10g | Saturated Fat: 8g | Sodium: 50mg | Fiber: 3g | Sugar: 16g

These blueberry oatmeal bars are a delicious and wholesome dessert that is perfect for an anti-inflammatory diet. Oats and whole wheat flour provide fiber and complex carbohydrates, while blueberries are rich in antioxidants and anti-inflammatory compounds. Honey adds a touch of natural sweetness without any refined sugar, and coconut oil is a healthy source of saturated fat. These bars are easy to make and can be enjoyed as a dessert or a snack. They can also be stored in an airtight container in the refrigerator for up to a week.

CHOCOLATE AVOCADO MOUSSE

10 minutes   0 minutes   4

Ingredients

- 2 ripe avocados
- 1/2 cup unsweetened cocoa powder
- 1/2 cup almond milk
- 1/4 cup maple syrup
- 1 tsp vanilla extract
- Pinch of salt
- Optional toppings: sliced strawberries, chopped nuts, whipped coconut cream

Preparation Steps

- Cut the avocados in half, remove the pit, and scoop the flesh into a blender or food processor.
- Add the cocoa powder, almond milk, maple syrup, vanilla extract, and salt to the blender with the avocado.
- Blend until the mixture is smooth and creamy, scraping down the sides as needed.
- Divide the mousse among 4 serving dishes or ramekins.
- Chill the mousse in the refrigerator for at least 30 minutes.
- Top with sliced strawberries, chopped nuts, or whipped coconut cream if desired.

Calories: 226 kcal | Carbohydrates: 24g | Protein: 4g | Fat: 16g | Saturated Fat: 4g | Sodium: 53mg | Fiber: 9g | Sugar: 11g

This chocolate avocado mousse is a decadent, healthy dessert with anti-inflammatory nutrients. The avocado provides healthy fats and fiber, while the cocoa powder is a rich source of flavonoids and antioxidants. Maple syrup adds natural sweetness without any refined sugar, and almond milk is a dairy-free alternative with low calories and high nutrients. This mousse is easy to make and can be prepared in advance for a quick and satisfying dessert. It's also a great way to get some extra nutrition for picky eaters who may not enjoy eating avocado alone.

GRILLED PINEAPPLE WITH CINNAMON AND HONEY

10 minutes   10 minutes   2

Ingredients

- 1 pineapple, cored and sliced into rounds
- 1 tablespoon coconut oil
- 1 teaspoon ground cinnamon
- 2 tablespoons honey
- Optional toppings: chopped nuts, coconut flakes

Preparation Steps

- Preheat a grill or grill pan to medium-high heat.
- In a small bowl, melt the coconut oil in the microwave or stove.
- Brush both sides of the pineapple slices with the melted coconut oil.
- Place the pineapple slices on the grill and cook for 2-3 minutes on each side until they are lightly charred and caramelized.
- In a small bowl, mix the cinnamon and honey.
- Drizzle the cinnamon-honey mixture over the grilled pineapple slices.
- Serve warm, topped with chopped nuts or coconut flakes if desired.

Calories: 140 kcal | Carbohydrates: 36g | Protein: 1g | Fat: 2g | Saturated Fat: 1g | Sodium: 2mg | Fiber: 3g | Sugar: 29g

This grilled pineapple dessert is a sweet and satisfying way to end a meal and provides anti-inflammatory nutrients. Pineapple contains the enzyme bromelain, which has been shown to reduce inflammation in the body. Cinnamon is a spice with anti-inflammatory properties, and honey provides natural sweetness without refined sugar. Grilling the pineapple brings natural sweetness and a delicious charred flavor. This dessert is quick and easy to make and can be customized with your favorite toppings like chopped nuts or coconut flakes.

BERRY CHIA SEED PUDDING

10 minutes   2 hours   4

Ingredients

- 1 cup unsweetened almond milk
- 1/2 cup plain Greek yogurt
- 1/4 cup chia seeds
- 1 tablespoon honey or maple syrup
- 1/2 teaspoon vanilla extract
- 1 cup mixed berries, fresh or frozen

Preparation Steps

- Whisk together the almond milk, Greek yogurt, chia seeds, honey or maple syrup, and vanilla extract in a mixing bowl until well combined.
- Stir in the mixed berries.
- Pour the mixture into individual serving jars or bowls.
- Cover and refrigerate for at least 2 hours or overnight until the chia seeds have absorbed the liquid, and the mixture has thickened.
- Serve the chilled chia seed pudding with additional berries on top.

Calories: 120 kcal | Carbohydrates: 14g | Protein: 6g | Fat: 5g | Saturated Fat: 1g | Sodium: 45mg | Fiber: 6g | Sugar: 7g

This berry chia seed pudding is a delicious, nutritious dessert with anti-inflammatory ingredients. Chia seeds are high in fiber and omega-3 fatty acids, both anti-inflammatory properties. Berries are rich in antioxidants, which can help reduce inflammation. Greek yogurt provides protein and creaminess to the pudding, while almond milk, honey, or maple syrup adds sweetness without refined sugar. This dessert is easy to make and can be prepared ahead of time for a healthy and satisfying treat.

BAKED APPLES WITH WALNUTS AND CINNAMON

10 minutes   40 minutes   4

Ingredients

- 4 medium-sized apples
- 1/4 cup chopped walnuts
- 1 teaspoon ground cinnamon
- 1 tablespoon honey or maple syrup
- 2 tablespoons unsalted butter or coconut oil, melted
- 1/4 cup water

Preparation Steps

- Preheat the oven to 375°F (190°C).
- Wash the apples and remove the core and seeds with a small knife or apple corer.
- Combine the chopped walnuts, ground cinnamon, and honey or maple syrup in a small mixing bowl.
- Stuff the mixture into the cavities of the apples.
- Place the apples in a baking dish and drizzle with melted butter or coconut oil.
- Pour water into the bottom of the dish.
- Bake for 35-40 minutes or until the apples are soft and tender.
- If desired, serve the warm baked apples with a scoop of vanilla ice cream or a dollop of Greek yogurt.

Calories: 170 kcal | Carbohydrates: 28g | Protein: 1g | Fat: 7g | Saturated Fat: 3g | Sodium: 5mg | Fiber: 5g | Sugar: 20g

These baked apples with walnuts and cinnamon are a cozy, comforting dessert with anti-inflammatory ingredients. Apples are rich in fiber and antioxidants, while walnuts provide healthy fats and protein. Cinnamon is a natural anti-inflammatory spice that adds warmth and flavor to the dish. Honey or maple syrup provides natural sweetness, and butter or coconut oil adds richness and depth of flavor. This dessert is easy to make and can be customized with your favorite toppings.

FROZEN YOGURT BARK WITH BERRIES AND NUTS

10 minutes • 4 hours • 6

Ingredients

- 2 cups plain Greek yogurt
- 2 tbsp honey
- 1 tsp vanilla extract
- 1 cup mixed berries (such as blueberries, raspberries, and strawberries)
- 1/4 cup chopped nuts (such as almonds or walnuts)

Preparation Steps

- Whisk together the Greek yogurt, honey, and vanilla extract in a bowl until well combined.
- Line a baking sheet with parchment paper and spread the yogurt mixture evenly onto the sheet.
- Sprinkle the mixed berries and chopped nuts over the yogurt mixture, pressing them gently into the yogurt with a spoon.
- Place the baking sheet in the freezer and freeze for at least 4 hours or until the yogurt is fully frozen.
- Once the yogurt is frozen, remove the baking sheet from the freezer and use a sharp knife to break the bark into small pieces.
- Serve immediately or store the bark in an airtight container in the freezer for up to 1 month.

Calories: 120 kcal | Carbohydrates: 13g | Protein: 8g | Fat: 4g | Saturated Fat: 1g | Sodium: 40mg | Fiber: 2g | Sugar: 10g

This frozen yogurt bark is a delicious and refreshing dessert packed with protein from Greek yogurt and healthy fats from nuts. The mixed berries boost antioxidants and fiber, while the honey adds a touch of sweetness. The bark is easy to make and can be stored in the freezer for a quick, healthy dessert or snack.

CHOCOLATE BANANA SMOOTHIE

🌿 5 minutes   ⏱ 0 minutes   🍴 1

Ingredients

- 1 ripe banana, sliced and frozen
- 1/2 cup unsweetened almond milk
- 1 tbsp unsweetened cocoa powder
- 1 tbsp almond butter
- 1 tsp honey (optional)
- Ice cubes (optional)

Preparation Steps

- Add the frozen banana, almond milk, cocoa powder, almond butter, and honey (if using) to a blender.
- Blend on high until smooth and creamy. If the smoothie is too thick, add a few ice cubes and blend again.
- Pour the smoothie into a glass and enjoy immediately.

Calories: 215 kcal | Carbohydrates: 27g | Protein: 5g | Fat: 12g | Saturated Fat: 1g | Sodium: 120mg | Fiber: 6g | Sugar: 14g

This chocolate banana smoothie is a satisfying and indulgent dessert packed with nutrients. The banana provides natural sweetness and potassium, while the cocoa powder adds a rich chocolate flavor and antioxidants. The almond milk and almond butter add protein and healthy fats, making the smoothie filling and satisfying. You can add a little honey or maple syrup if you prefer a sweeter smoothie. This smoothie is best enjoyed immediately, but you can store any leftovers in the fridge for up to 24 hours.

LEMON POPPY SEED CAKE RECIPE

20 minutes   45 minutes   10

Ingredients

For the cake:
- 1 cup almond flour
- 1/2 cup coconut flour
- 1/2 cup unsweetened applesauce
- 1/3 cup maple syrup
- 1/3 cup melted coconut oil
- 3 large eggs

- 1 teaspoon baking powder
- 1 tablespoon poppy seeds
- 1 tablespoon lemon zest
- 1/2 teaspoon baking soda
- 1/4 teaspoon salt

For the glaze:
- 1/4 cup lemon juice
- 1/4 cup coconut cream
- 2 tablespoons honey

Preparation Steps

- Preheat the oven to 350°F (180°C). Grease an 8-inch cake pan with coconut oil.
- Mix the almond flour, coconut flour, poppy seeds, lemon zest, baking powder, baking soda, and salt in a large bowl.
- Whisk together the eggs, applesauce, maple syrup, and melted coconut oil in a separate bowl.
- Add the wet ingredients to the dry ingredients and mix until well combined.
- Pour the batter into the prepared cake pan and bake for 40-45 minutes, or until a toothpick inserted in the center of the cake comes out clean.
- While the cake is baking, make the glaze by whisking together the lemon juice, coconut cream, and honey.
- Once the cake is made, remove it from the oven and let it cool for a few minutes.
- Drizzle the glaze over the cake while it is still warm.
- Let the cake cool completely before slicing and serving.

Calories: 240 kcal | Carbohydrates: 18g | Protein: 6g | Fat: 17g | Saturated Fat: 10g | Cholesterol: 56mg | Sodium: 155mg | Fiber: 4g | Sugar: 10g

This Lemon Poppy Seed Cake is a delicious and wholesome dessert option incorporating anti-inflammatory ingredients such as almond flour, coconut oil, and lemon. The cake is also gluten-free and dairy-free, making it suitable for those with dietary restrictions. Adding poppy seeds adds a satisfying crunch, while the lemon glaze provides a zesty and sweet finish. Enjoy a slice as a dessert or as a snack any time of the day.

SWEET POTATO BROWNIES
20 minutes   30 minutes   9

Ingredients

- 1 cup mashed sweet potatoes (about 2 medium sweet potatoes)
- 1/2 cup almond flour
- 1/4 cup cocoa powder
- 1/4 cup maple syrup
- 2 eggs
- 1/4 cup coconut oil, melted
- 1 tsp vanilla extract
- 1/2 tsp baking powder
- 1/4 tsp salt
- 1/2 cup dark chocolate chips

Preparation Steps

- Preheat oven to 350°F (175°C). Line an 8-inch square baking dish with parchment paper.
- Pierce sweet potatoes with a fork several times, then microwave for 5-7 minutes or until soft.
- Let cool, then peel and mash the sweet potatoes in a bowl.
- Whisk together almond flour, cocoa powder, baking powder, and salt in a separate bowl.
- Beat eggs, maple syrup, melted coconut oil, and vanilla extract in another bowl.
- Add the dry ingredients to the wet ingredients and mix well.
- Fold in the mashed sweet potatoes and chocolate chips.
- Pour the mixture into the prepared baking dish and smooth the top with a spatula.
- Bake for 25-30 minutes or until a toothpick inserted in the center comes clean.
- Let the brownies cool in the baking dish for 10 minutes, then transfer them to a wire rack to cool completely.

Calories: 206 kcal | Carbohydrates: 17g | Protein: 4g | Fat: 15g | Saturated Fat: 8g | Sodium: 78mg | Fiber: 3g | Sugar: 8g

These sweet potato brownies are a healthier alternative to traditional brownies, thanks to the nutrient-dense sweet potatoes and almond flour. They are naturally sweetened with maple syrup and loaded with dark chocolate chips for a rich and decadent flavor. The anti-inflammatory properties of sweet potatoes and dark chocolate make these brownies a guilt-free indulgence.

PUMPKIN SPICE OATMEAL COOKIES

10 minutes   15 minutes   12

Ingredients

- 1 cup rolled oats
- 1/2 cup almond flour
- 1/4 cup pumpkin puree
- 1/4 cup pure maple syrup
- 1/4 cup coconut oil, melted
- 1 egg
- 1 tsp baking powder
- 1 tsp vanilla extract
- 1 tsp cinnamon
- 1/2 tsp ground ginger
- 1/4 tsp nutmeg
- 1/4 tsp salt
- 1/2 cup chopped pecans (optional)

Preparation Steps

- Preheat the oven to 350°F and line a baking sheet with parchment paper.
- Mix the rolled oats, almond flour, baking powder, cinnamon, ginger, nutmeg, and salt in a large bowl.
- Whisk together the pumpkin puree, maple syrup, melted coconut oil, egg, and vanilla extract in a separate bowl.
- Pour the wet ingredients into the dry ingredients and stir until well combined. Fold in the chopped pecans, if using.
- Use a cookie scoop or tablespoon to drop dough onto the prepared baking sheet, spacing the cookies about 2 inches apart.
- Bake for 12-15 minutes until the edges are golden brown and the centers are set.
- Remove from the oven and cool on the baking sheet for 5 minutes, then transfer to a wire rack to cool completely.

Calories: 155 kcal | Carbohydrates: 12g | Protein: 3g | Fat: 11g | Saturated Fat: 5g | Sodium: 67mg | Fiber: 2g | Sugar: 5g

These pumpkin spice oatmeal cookies are a healthy and delicious way to satisfy your sweet tooth. The combination of pumpkin puree, spices, and pure maple syrup gives these cookies a warm and cozy flavor. Plus, the rolled oats and almond flour add fiber and protein to keep you feeling full and satisfied. Enjoy them as a snack or a dessert, and store any leftovers in an airtight container for up to 5 days.

CHAPTER 13
VEGETARIAN

LENTIL AND VEGETABLE STIR-FRY

🌿 10 minutes ⏱ 25 minutes 🍽 4

Ingredients

- 1 cup of lentils, rinsed and drained
- 2 cups of water
- 1 tablespoon olive oil
- 1 onion, chopped
- 2 cloves garlic, minced
- 1 red bell pepper, sliced
- 1 small head of broccoli, chopped into floret

- 1 medium carrot, sliced
- 1 tablespoon of freshly grated ginger
- 1 tablespoon of soy sauce
- 1 tablespoon of honey
- 1 green bell pepper, sliced
- 1 teaspoon of sriracha sauce
- 1 tablespoon of sesame oil
- 1 tablespoon of sesame seeds
- Fresh cilantro for garnish (optional)

Preparation Steps

- Cook lentils according to package directions until tender.
- In a large skillet or wok, heat olive oil over medium-high heat. Add onion and garlic, and sauté for 2-3 minutes until fragrant.
- Add the bell peppers, broccoli, and carrot to the skillet or wok, and sauté for 5-7 minutes until the vegetables are slightly softened.
- Stir in the ginger, soy sauce, honey, sriracha sauce, and sesame oil until well combined.
- Add the cooked lentils to the skillet or wok, and stir to combine with the vegetables and sauce. Cook for an additional 3-5 minutes until heated through.
- Season with salt and pepper to taste.
- If desired, sprinkle sesame seeds over the top of the stir-fry and garnish with fresh cilantro.

Calories: 292 kcal | Carbohydrates: 47g | Protein: 16g | Fat: 5g | Saturated Fat: 1g | Sodium: 367mg | Fiber: 16g | Sugar: 11g

This lentil and vegetable stir-fry is a great way to add protein and fiber to your diet. The lentils are a fantastic source of plant-based protein, while the colorful veggies provide an array of vitamins and minerals. The sweet and savory sauce adds excellent flavor to the dish. Serve it over brown rice or quinoa for a complete meal.

CHICKPEA AND SPINACH CURRY

10 minutes   25 minutes   4

Ingredients

- 1 tablespoon coconut oil
- 1 onion, diced
- 3 garlic cloves, minced
- 1 tablespoon grated ginger
- 1 tablespoon curry powder
- 1/2 teaspoon ground turmeric
- 1/4 teaspoon ground cinnamon

- 1/4 teaspoon cayenne pepper
- 1 can chickpeas, drained and rinsed
- 1 can dice tomatoes
- 1/2 cup vegetable broth
- 4 cups fresh spinach
- Salt and pepper, to taste (optional)
- Optional: chopped fresh cilantro for garnish

Preparation Steps

- Heat coconut oil in a large skillet over medium heat. Add onion, garlic, and ginger, and cook for 2-3 minutes until the onion is translucent.
- Add curry powder, turmeric, cinnamon, and cayenne pepper to the skillet and cook for 1-2 minutes until fragrant.
- Add chickpeas, diced tomatoes, and vegetable broth to the skillet. Bring to a simmer and cook for 10-15 minutes until the sauce thickens and the chickpeas are heated through.
- Stir in the spinach and let it wilt down for a few minutes—season with salt and pepper to taste.
- Serve the curry hot, garnished with fresh cilantro if desired. It can be served on its own or over brown rice for a heartier meal.

Calories: 206 kcal | Carbohydrates: 33g | Protein: 10g | Fat: 5g | Saturated Fat: 3g | Sodium: 509mg | Fiber: 9g | Sugar: 8g

This chickpea and spinach curry is a great way to incorporate more plant-based protein and anti-inflammatory ingredients into your diet. Chickpeas are rich in protein and fiber, while spinach is packed with vitamins and minerals. The flavorful spices add a delicious depth of flavor, and the dish can easily be customized to your preferred spice level. This recipe is also vegan and gluten-free, making it an excellent option for those with dietary restrictions

QUINOA AND VEGETABLE STUFFED PEPPERS

20 minutes   40 minutes   4

Ingredients

- 4 bell peppers
- 1 cup quinoa, rinsed and drained
- 2 cups vegetable broth
- 1 tbsp olive oil
- 1 onion, chopped
- 2 garlic cloves, minced

- 1 zucchini, diced
- 1 red bell pepper, diced
- 1 carrot, diced
- 1 tsp cumin
- 1 tsp smoked paprika
- 1/4 tsp cayenne pepper
- Salt and pepper, to taste (optional)
- 1/2 cup grated Parmesan cheese

Preparation Steps

- Preheat the oven to 375°F (190°C). Cut the tops off the bell peppers and remove the seeds and membranes. Place the peppers in a baking dish and set aside.
- Bring the quinoa and vegetable broth to a boil in a medium saucepan. Reduce heat to low and simmer for 15-20 minutes until the quinoa is tender and the broth is absorbed.
- In a large skillet, heat the olive oil over medium heat. Add the onion, garlic, and sauté for 2-3 minutes or until the onion is translucent.
- Add the zucchini, carrot, and red bell pepper to the skillet and sauté for 5-7 minutes, or until the vegetables are tender.
- Stir in the cooked quinoa, cumin, smoked paprika, cayenne pepper, salt, and pepper. Cook for 2-3 minutes or until the spices are fragrant.
- Spoon the quinoa and vegetable mixture into the bell peppers, dividing it evenly among the four peppers. Sprinkle Parmesan cheese on top, if desired.
- Cover the baking dish with foil and bake for 25-30 minutes until the peppers are tender and the filling is heated.

Calories: 310kcal | Carbohydrates: 34g | Protein: 10g | Fat: 16g | Saturated Fat: 4g | Cholesterol: 17mg | Sodium: 299mg | Fiber: 7g | Sugar: 6g

These quinoa and vegetable stuffed peppers are a delicious and colorful way to enjoy a variety of anti-inflammatory veggies. Quinoa adds a protein boost and helps keep you full, while the spices provide a warm and savory flavor. These peppers can be made ahead of time and reheated for an easy meal during the week. Adding Parmesan cheese is optional but adds a nice touch of umami flavor.

ROASTED ROOT VEGETABLES WITH TAHINI SAUCE

🌿 10 minutes   ⏱ 35 minutes   🍴 4

Ingredients

For the roasted vegetables:

- 1 large sweet potato, peeled and chopped into small cubes
- 2 parsnips, peeled and chopped into small cubes
- 2 carrots, peeled and chopped into small cubes
- 1 red onion, sliced
- 2 tbsp olive oil
- 1 tsp ground cumin

- 1 tsp ground coriander
- Salt and pepper, to taste (optional)

For the tahini sauce:

- 1/4 cup tahini
- 2 tbsp lemon juice
- 2 tbsp water
- 1 garlic clove, minced
- Salt and pepper, to taste (optional)

Preparation Steps

- Preheat the oven to 400°F (200°C).
- In a large bowl, toss the chopped sweet potato, parsnips, carrots, and red onion with olive oil, cumin, coriander, salt, and pepper.
- Spread the vegetables in a single layer on a baking sheet and roast for 30-35 minutes or until tender and lightly browned.
- While the vegetables are roasting, make the tahini sauce. Whisk together the tahini, lemon juice, water, minced garlic, salt, and pepper in a small bowl until smooth and creamy.
- Serve the roasted root vegetables with a dollop of tahini sauce on top.

Calories: 234 kcal | Carbohydrates: 28g | Protein: 5g | Fat: 13g | Saturated Fat: 2g | Sodium: 94mg | Fiber: 6g | Sugar: 8g

This dish is a delicious and filling way to incorporate a variety of colorful and anti-inflammatory root vegetables into your diet. The roasting process brings out the natural sweetness of the vegetables and enhances their flavor, while the tahini sauce adds a creamy and tangy element. The dish is high in fiber and plant-based protein from vegetables and tahini, making it a nutritious and satisfying meal.

TOFU AND VEGETABLE KEBABS

20 minutes　　10 minutes　　4

Ingredients

- 1 block of extra-firm tofu, pressed and cut into cubes
- 1 red bell pepper, chopped into bite-sized pieces
- 1 yellow bell pepper, chopped into bite-sized pieces
- 1 zucchini, sliced into rounds
- 1/4 cup olive oil
- 1 red onion, chopped into bite-sized pieces
- 2 tbsp balsamic vinegar
- 1 tbsp honey or maple syrup
- 1 tsp dried oregano
- 1/2 tsp garlic powder
- Salt and pepper, to taste (optional)

Preparation Steps

- Preheat the grill or grill pan to medium-high heat.
- Thread tofu, peppers, zucchini, and onion onto skewers.
- Whisk together olive oil, balsamic vinegar, honey or maple syrup, oregano, garlic powder, salt, and pepper in a small bowl.
- Brush the marinade onto the kebabs, making sure all sides are coated.
- Grill the kebabs for 10-15 minutes, flipping once halfway through until the tofu is slightly browned and the vegetables are tender.
- Serve hot, and enjoy!

Calories: 236 kcal | Carbohydrates: 14g | Protein: 12g | Fat: 16g | Saturated Fat: 2g | Sodium: 28mg | Fiber: 3g | Sugar: 10g

These tofu and vegetable kebabs are a tasty and colorful way to enjoy a protein-packed meal while incorporating a variety of anti-inflammatory vegetables. The marinade adds a tangy and sweet flavor, while the tofu adds a satisfying and meaty texture. This dish can be enjoyed as a main course or a side dish to complement other dishes. It can also be easily adapted to veganism using maple syrup instead of honey.

BLACK BEAN AND SWEET POTATO CHILI

15 minutes • 30 minutes • 6

Ingredients

- 1 tbsp olive oil
- 1 onion, chopped
- 3 garlic cloves, minced
- 2 sweet potatoes, peeled and diced
- 1 red bell pepper, chopped
- 2 tsp chili powder
- 1 tsp cumin
- 1/2 tsp smoked paprika
- 1/4 tsp cayenne pepper
- Salt and pepper, to taste (optional)
- 1 can (14 oz) diced tomatoes
- 2 cans (15 oz each) of black beans, rinsed and drained
- 2 cups vegetable broth
- 1 lime, juiced
- Optional toppings: avocado, cilantro, diced red onion

Preparation Steps

- In a large pot, heat the olive oil over medium heat. Add the onion, garlic, and sauté for 2-3 minutes or until the onion is translucent.
- Add the sweet potatoes and red bell pepper to the pot and sauté for 5-7 minutes, or until the vegetables are slightly tender.
- Add the chili powder, cumin, smoked paprika, cayenne pepper, salt, and pepper to the pot and stir to combine.
- Pour in the diced tomatoes, black beans, and vegetable broth. Stir well and bring the mixture to a simmer.
- Cover the pot and let the chili simmer for 20-25 minutes, or until the sweet potatoes are fork-tender and the flavors have melded together.
- Stir in the lime juice and season with additional salt and pepper, if needed.
- Serve hot and top with optional toppings, if desired.

Calories: 236 kcal | Carbohydrates: 43g | Protein: 11g | Fat: 3g | Saturated Fat: 1g | Sodium: 807mg | Fiber: 13g | Sugar: 8g

This black bean and sweet potato chili is comforting and satisfying for a cozy night. The combination of black beans and sweet potatoes creates a deliciously hearty texture, while the spices add warmth and depth of flavor. This recipe is naturally vegetarian and vegan, with anti-inflammatory ingredients to support your overall health and well-being. Enjoy with your favorite toppings, such as avocado, cilantro, and diced red onion.

SPAGHETTI SQUASH WITH ROASTED TOMATOES

10 minutes   40 minutes   4

Ingredients

- 1 medium spaghetti squash
- 2 cups cherry tomatoes, halved
- 2 cloves garlic, minced
- 2 tbsp olive oil
- Salt and pepper, to taste (optional)
- 1/4 cup fresh basil, chopped
- Optional: grated Parmesan cheese

Preparation Steps

- Preheat the oven to 375°F (190°C).
- Cut the spaghetti squash in half lengthwise and scoop out the seeds. Drizzle with olive oil and season with salt and pepper.
- Place the squash cut-side on a baking sheet and roast for 30-40 minutes, or until the flesh is tender and easily separated into strands with a fork.
- In the meantime, toss the cherry tomatoes and garlic with 1 tbsp of olive oil and a pinch of salt and pepper. Spread them on a separate baking sheet and roast for 15-20 minutes or until the tomatoes are soft and slightly caramelized.
- Once the spaghetti squash is done, use a fork to scrape out the strands and place them in a serving bowl.
- Top the squash with the roasted tomatoes and garlic, and sprinkle with fresh basil. Add grated Parmesan cheese, if desired.
- Serve hot, and enjoy!

Calories: 130 kcal | Carbohydrates: 17g | Protein: 2g | Fat: 7g | Saturated Fat: 1g | Sodium: 30mg | Fiber: 4g | Sugar: 6g

This spaghetti squash with roasted tomatoes and basil is a light and flavorful dish perfect for a healthy, anti-inflammatory meal. Spaghetti squash is an excellent alternative to traditional pasta, and it pairs perfectly with the roasted tomatoes' sweetness and the basil's freshness. This dish is low in calories and high in fiber, making it an excellent option for weight management and overall health.

CAULIFLOWER AND CHICKPEA CURRY

🌿 10 minutes   ⏱ 30 minutes   🍽 4

Ingredients

- 1 large head of cauliflower, chopped
- 1 can chickpeas, drained and rinsed
- 3 cloves garlic, minced
- 1 tbsp olive oil
- 1 tbsp curry powder
- 1 tsp ground cumin
- 1 tsp ground coriander
- 1/2 tsp turmeric
- 1 onion, diced
- 1/4 tsp cayenne pepper
- 1 can (14 oz) diced tomatoes
- 1 can (13.5 oz) full-fat coconut milk
- 1/4 cup chopped fresh cilantro
- Salt and pepper, to taste (optional)
- Cooked brown rice or quinoa for serving

Preparation Steps

- In a large skillet, heat the olive oil over medium heat. Add the onion, garlic, and sauté for 2-3 minutes or until the onion is translucent.
- Add the cauliflower and chickpeas to the skillet and stir to combine.
- Add the curry powder, cumin, coriander, turmeric, and cayenne pepper to the skillet and stir to coat the vegetables.
- Pour the diced tomatoes and coconut milk over the vegetables and stir to combine.
- Reduce heat to low and simmer for 20-25 minutes until the cauliflower is tender and the sauce has thickened.
- Stir in the chopped cilantro and season with salt and pepper to taste.
- Serve the curry over cooked brown rice or quinoa.

Calories: 331 kcal | Carbohydrates: 35g | Protein: 11g | Fat: 20g | Saturated Fat: 14g | Sodium: 655mg | Fiber: 10g | Sugar: 11g

This cauliflower and chickpea curry is a delicious and satisfying way to enjoy the anti-inflammatory benefits of these two ingredients. The creamy coconut milk-based sauce is flavored with a mix of warm and fragrant spices, and the dish is finished with fresh cilantro for a burst of flavor. Serve it over a brown rice or quinoa bed for a complete and nutritious meal.

EGGPLANT AND ZUCCHINI LASAGNA

 30 minutes 1 hour 🍽 8

Ingredients

- 1 eggplant, sliced lengthwise
- 1 zucchini, sliced lengthwise
- 1 can (28 oz) crushed tomatoes
- 1 tsp dried basil
- 1 tsp dried oregano
- Salt and pepper, to taste (optional)
- 1 cup ricotta cheese
- 1/2 cup grated Parmesan cheese
- 12 lasagna noodles, cooked according to package instructions
- 1 cup shredded mozzarella cheese

Preparation Steps

- Preheat the oven to 375°F (190°C).
- Place the eggplant and zucchini slices on a baking sheet lined with parchment paper. Brush with olive oil and season with salt and pepper. Roast for 25-30 minutes or until tender.
- Mix the ricotta and Parmesan cheese in a mixing bowl and season with salt and pepper. Mix well.
- To assemble the lasagna, spread a thin layer of crushed tomatoes on the bottom of a 9x13-inch baking dish. Top with 3 lasagna noodles, followed by a layer of roasted eggplant and zucchini, a layer of ricotta mixture, and a layer of mozzarella cheese.
- Repeat until all ingredients are used up, finishing with a layer of crushed tomatoes and mozzarella cheese on top.
- Cover with foil and bake for 30 minutes. Remove the foil and bake for 15-20 minutes or until the cheese is melted and bubbly.
- Let cool for a few minutes before serving.

Calories: 310kcal | Carbohydrates: 34g | Protein: 10g | Fat: 16g | Saturated Fat: 4g | Cholesterol: 17mg | Sodium: 299mg | Fiber: 7g | Sugar: 6g

This eggplant and zucchini lasagna is a delicious and healthy alternative to traditional lasagna. The roasted vegetables add a rich and savory flavor, while the ricotta mixture provides a creamy and decadent texture. This dish is perfect for a cozy family dinner or as a meal prep option for the week. Plus, it's packed with anti-inflammatory ingredients like eggplant and zucchini to support overall health and well-being.

SWEET POTATO AND KALE HASH

15 minutes   25 minutes   4

Ingredients

- 2 large sweet potatoes, peeled and diced
- 1 large onion, chopped
- 2 garlic cloves, minced
- 1 bunch of kale, stems removed and chopped
- 2 tbsp olive oil
- 1 tsp smoked paprika
- 1/2 tsp cumin
- Salt and pepper, to taste (optional)
- 4 eggs (optional)

Preparation Steps

- Preheat oven to 375°F (190°C).
- Heat olive oil in a large skillet over medium heat. Add chopped onion and minced garlic, and cook for 2-3 minutes or until the onion is translucent.
- Add diced sweet potatoes, smoked paprika, cumin, salt, and pepper to the skillet. Cook for 10-12 minutes or until sweet potatoes are tender and slightly browned.
- Add chopped kale to the skillet and cook for 5-7 minutes or until kale is wilted and tender.
- Remove from heat and divide the mixture into 4 bowls.
- Optional: crack an egg on top of each bowl of hash.
- Bake in preheated oven for 10-12 minutes or until the eggs are cooked to your desired level of doneness.
- Serve hot, and enjoy!

Calories: 246 kcal | Carbohydrates: 31g | Protein: 7g | Fat: 12g | Saturated Fat: 2g | Sodium: 83mg | Fiber: 6g | Sugar: 7g

This Sweet Potato and Kale Hash is a filling and delicious breakfast option that provides a variety of nutrients and anti-inflammatory ingredients. Sweet potatoes are a great source of fiber, potassium, and vitamin A, while kale boosts vitamin C and antioxidants. Adding an egg on top provides protein to keep you full and satisfied throughout the morning.

CHAPTER 14
SALAD

GRILLED CHICKEN AND AVOCADO SALAD

🌿 10 minutes ⏱ 15 minutes 🍴 4

Ingredients

For the Salad:
- 4 chicken breasts
- Salt and pepper, to taste (optional)
- 2 tablespoons olive oil
- 8 cups mixed greens
- 2 avocados, diced
- 1 red onion, thinly sliced
- 1 cup cherry tomatoes, halved

- 1/4 cup chopped cilantro

For the Dressing:
- 1/4 cup freshly squeezed lime juice
- 2 tablespoons honey
- 2 tablespoons chopped cilantro
- 1 garlic clove, minced
- 1/4 cup olive oil
- Salt and pepper, to taste (optional)

Preparation Steps

- Preheat the grill or grill pan to medium-high heat.
- Season chicken breasts with salt and pepper, and drizzle with olive oil. Grill for 5-6 minutes per side or until cooked through. Remove from grill and let rest for 5 minutes before slicing.
- Combine mixed greens, diced avocado, sliced red onion, halved cherry tomatoes, and chopped cilantro in a large bowl.
- Whisk together lime juice, honey, chopped cilantro, minced garlic, olive oil, salt, and pepper in a small bowl.
- Pour dressing over the salad and toss until well coated.
- Divide salad onto four plates, and top with sliced grilled chicken.
- Serve and enjoy!

Calories: 450 kcal | Carbohydrates: 22g | Protein: 35g | Fat: 26g | Saturated Fat: 4g | Sodium: 140mg | Fiber: 8g | Sugar: 11g

This Grilled Chicken and Avocado Salad with Cilantro-Lime Dressing is a delicious and satisfying way to incorporate anti-inflammatory ingredients into your diet. Grilled chicken and avocado provide protein and healthy fats, while the mixed greens, red onion, and cherry tomatoes are rich in vitamins and minerals. The dressing is made with fresh lime juice and cilantro, giving it a bright and zesty flavor. It's a perfect lunch or dinner option that's easy to make and great for meal prep.

RAINBOW SALAD WITH TURMERIC DRESSING

🌿 15 minutes   ⏱ 0 minutes   🍴 4

Ingredients

For the salad:

- 6 cups mixed greens (spinach, kale, lettuce)
- 1 red bell pepper, sliced
- 1 yellow bell pepper, sliced
- 1 orange bell pepper, sliced
- 2 medium carrots, julienned
- 1/4 head of red cabbage, thinly sliced
- 1 avocado, sliced

- 1/4 cup chopped fresh cilantro
- 1/4 cup chopped cashews or almonds

For the dressing:

- 1/4 cup olive oil
- 2 tablespoons apple cider vinegar
- 1 tablespoon honey
- 1 tablespoon fresh lemon juice
- 1 teaspoon ground turmeric
- 1/2 teaspoon ground cumin
- 1/4 teaspoon garlic powder
- Salt and pepper, to taste (optional)

Preparation Steps

- In a large bowl, combine the mixed greens, sliced bell peppers, julienned carrots, and sliced red cabbage.
- In a separate small bowl, whisk together the olive oil, apple cider vinegar, honey, lemon juice, ground turmeric, ground cumin, garlic powder, salt, and pepper to make the dressing.
- Drizzle the dressing over the salad and toss to coat.
- Top the salad with sliced avocado, chopped cilantro, and chopped cashews or almonds.

> Calories: 277 kcal | Carbohydrates: 22g | Protein: 5g | Fat: 22g | Saturated Fat: 3g | Sodium: 47mg | Fiber: 7g | Sugar: 12g

This Rainbow Salad with Turmeric Dressing is not only beautiful to look at but it's also packed with nutrients and anti-inflammatory ingredients. Combining mixed greens, bell peppers, carrots, red cabbage, avocado, and nuts creates a satisfying crunch and an explosion of flavors in your mouth. The turmeric dressing is the perfect finishing touch, adding subtle spiciness and a pop of color to the salad. This salad can be served as a light lunch or a refreshing side dish for any meal.

WATERMELON AND FETA SALAD WITH MINT

15 minutes   0 minutes   4

Ingredients

- 4 cups cubed watermelon
- 1/2 cup crumbled feta cheese
- 1/4 cup chopped fresh mint
- 1 tbsp extra-virgin olive oil
- 1 tbsp balsamic vinegar
- Salt and pepper, to taste (optional)

Preparation Steps

- Combine the cubed watermelon, crumbled feta cheese, and chopped fresh mint in a large mixing bowl.
- Whisk together the extra-virgin olive oil, balsamic vinegar, salt, and pepper in a separate small mixing bowl.
- Drizzle the dressing over the watermelon salad and gently toss to combine.
- Serve chilled, and enjoy!

Calories: 120 kcal | Carbohydrates: 10g | Protein: 3g | Fat: 8g | Saturated Fat: 3g | Sodium: 190mg | Fiber: 1g | Sugar: 8g

This watermelon and feta salad is a refreshing and flavorful way to enjoy anti-inflammatory ingredients like watermelon and fresh mint. Adding tangy feta cheese, simple olive oil, and balsamic vinegar dressing provides a delicious balance of flavors. This salad is perfect for summer picnics, barbecues or as a light and healthy side dish.

QUINOA AND ROASTED VEGETABLE SALAD

🌿 15 minutes   ⏱ 30 minutes   🍴 4

Ingredients

- 1 cup quinoa, rinsed and drained
- 2 cups vegetable broth
- 2 cups mixed vegetables chopped
- 1 tbsp olive oil
- 1 tsp dried thyme
- 1 tsp dried oregano

- 1/4 tsp garlic powder
- Salt and pepper, to taste (optional)
- 2 tbsp lemon juice
- 1 tbsp Dijon mustard
- 1 tbsp honey or maple syrup
- 3 tbsp olive oil
- 2 tbsp fresh parsley, chopped
- 2 tbsp fresh basil, chopped

Preparation Steps

- Preheat the oven to 400°F (200°C). Line a baking sheet with parchment paper.
- Bring the quinoa and vegetable broth to a boil in a medium saucepan. Reduce heat to low and simmer for 15-20 minutes until the quinoa is tender and the broth is absorbed.
- While the quinoa is cooking, toss the mixed vegetables with olive oil, thyme, oregano, garlic powder, salt, and pepper, to taste. Spread the vegetables on the prepared baking sheet and roast for 20-25 minutes or until tender and slightly charred.
- Whisk together the lemon juice, Dijon mustard, honey or maple syrup, and olive oil in a small bowl—season with salt and pepper to taste.
- Combine the cooked quinoa, roasted vegetables, and dressing in a large bowl. Toss to combine.
- Garnish with fresh parsley and basil before serving.

Calories: 327 kcal | Carbohydrates: 37g | Protein: 7g | Fat: 18g | Saturated Fat: 2g | Sodium: 488mg | Fiber: 6g | Sugar: 10g

This quinoa and roasted vegetable salad is a delicious and filling way to enjoy a variety of anti-inflammatory veggies. The quinoa boosts the protein and helps keep you full, while the roasted vegetables provide a delightful, caramelized flavor. The tangy dressing made with lemon juice and Dijon mustard ties everything together and adds an extra kick of flavor. This salad can be a primary or side dish alongside grilled chicken or fish.

TUNA AND WHITE BEAN SALAD WITH LEMON

10 minutes   0 minutes   4

Ingredients

- 2 cans (5 oz each) of tuna in water, drained
- 1 can (15 oz) of white beans, rinsed and drained
- 1/2 red onion, thinly sliced
- 1/2 red bell pepper, diced
- 2 tbsp fresh dill, chopped
- 1 celery stalk, thinly sliced
- 1/4 cup fresh lemon juice
- 1/4 cup extra-virgin olive oil
- Salt and pepper, to taste (optional)
- 4 cups mixed salad greens

Preparation Steps

- Combine the tuna, white beans, red onion, red bell pepper, celery, and dill in a large mixing bowl.
- Whisk together the lemon juice, olive oil, salt, and pepper in a small mixing bowl.
- Pour the dressing over the tuna and white bean mixture and stir until evenly coated.
- Serve the tuna and white bean salad over a bed of mixed salad greens.
- Enjoy!

Calories: 337 kcal | Carbohydrates: 26g | Protein: 26g | Fat: 15g | Saturated Fat: 2g | Sodium: 391mg | Fiber: 7g | Sugar: 2g

This tuna and white bean salad is a quick and easy way to incorporate anti-inflammatory foods into your diet. Tuna and white beans provide a great source of protein, while the lemon and dill dressing gives the salad a bright and refreshing flavor. The mixed greens offer additional vitamins and minerals, making this salad nutritious and satisfying.

MIXED GREENS SALAD WITH STRAWBERRIES

10 minutes   10 minutes   4

Ingredients

For the Salad:
- 6 cups mixed greens
- 1-pint strawberries, sliced
- 1/2 cup crumbled goat cheese
- 1/4 cup sliced almonds (optional)

For the Dressing:
- 2 tablespoons balsamic vinegar
- 1 tablespoon honey
- 1/4 cup olive oil
- Salt and pepper to taste (optional)

Preparation Steps

- Combine the mixed greens, sliced strawberries, crumbled goat cheese, and sliced almonds in a large bowl.
- Whisk together the balsamic vinegar, honey, olive oil, salt, and pepper in a small bowl until emulsified.
- Drizzle the dressing over the salad and toss until evenly coated.
- Serve immediately and enjoy!

Calories: 200 kcal | Carbohydrates: 10g | Protein: 5g | Fat: 16g | Saturated Fat: 4g | Cholesterol: 9mg | Sodium: 135mg | Fiber: 3g | Sugar: 6g

This Mixed Greens Salad with Strawberries and Goat Cheese is a light and refreshing way to enjoy a variety of anti-inflammatory ingredients. The sweet strawberries and tangy goat cheese pair perfectly with the simple balsamic vinaigrette, while the sliced almonds add a nice crunch. This salad can be enjoyed as a light lunch or as a side dish with dinner.

SHRIMP AND MANGO SALAD WITH AVOCADO

🌿 15 minutes ⏱ 5 minutes 🍴 4

Ingredients

For the salad:
- 1 lb. shrimp, peeled and deveined
- 1 mango, peeled and diced
- 1 avocado, peeled and diced
- 1 red bell pepper, diced
- 4 cups mixed greens
- 1/4 cup chopped fresh cilantro
- Salt and pepper, to taste

- Lime wedges for serving

For the dressing:
- 1 avocado, peeled and pitted
- 1/4 cup plain Greek yogurt
- 1/4 cup fresh lime juice
- 2 garlic cloves, minced
- 1/4 cup chopped fresh cilantro
- Salt and pepper, to taste (optional)
- Water, as needed

Preparation Steps

- Combine the shrimp, mango, avocado, red bell pepper, mixed greens, and cilantro in a large bowl—season with salt and pepper to taste.
- Place the avocado, Greek yogurt, lime juice, garlic, cilantro, salt, and pepper in a blender or food processor to make the dressing. Blend until smooth. Add water as needed to thin the sauce to your desired consistency.
- Heat a large skillet over medium-high heat. Add the shrimp and cook for 2-3 minutes per side until pink and cooked through.
- Divide the salad among four plates. Top each dish with the cooked shrimp and a drizzle of the avocado dressing. Serve with lime wedges.

Calories: 306 kcal | Carbohydrates: 21g | Protein: 26g | Fat: 14g | Saturated Fat: 2g | Cholesterol: 229mg | Sodium: 327mg | Fiber: 9g | Sugar: 8g

This shrimp and mango salad with avocado dressing is a tropical and refreshing way to enjoy anti-inflammatory ingredients. Shrimp provides lean protein, while mango adds sweetness and vitamin C. The creamy avocado dressing is a healthier alternative to traditional dressings and complements the flavors of the salad well. This salad is perfect for a light lunch or dinner during warmer months.

GREEK SALAD WITH GRILLED CHICKEN

🌿 15 minutes   ⏱ 15 minutes   🍽 4

Ingredients

For the salad:
- 1 lb. boneless, skinless chicken breasts
- 1 tsp dried oregano
- 1/2 tsp garlic powder
- 1/4 tsp salt
- 1/4 tsp black pepper
- 4 cups mixed greens
- 2 cups cherry tomatoes, halved
- 1 cucumber, sliced
- 1/2 red onion, sliced
- 1/2 cup kalamata olives, pitted
- 1/2 cup crumbled feta cheese

For the dressing:
- 1/4 cup extra-virgin olive oil
- 2 tbsp red wine vinegar
- 1 clove garlic, minced
- 1 tsp dried oregano
- 1/4 tsp salt
- 1/4 tsp black pepper

Preparation Steps

- Preheat a grill or grill pan to medium-high heat. Season the chicken breasts with oregano, garlic powder, salt, and black pepper.
- Grill the chicken for 6-8 minutes per side or until the internal temperature reaches 165°F. Set aside to rest for 5 minutes before slicing.
- Combine the mixed greens, cherry tomatoes, cucumber, red onion, kalamata olives, and feta cheese in a large bowl.
- Whisk together the olive oil, red wine vinegar, garlic, oregano, salt, and black pepper in a small bowl to make the dressing.
- Drizzle the dressing over the salad and toss to combine.
- Top the salad with the sliced grilled chicken and serve immediately.

Calories: 435 kcal | Carbohydrates: 14g | Protein: 38g | Fat: 26g | Saturated Fat: 6g | Cholesterol: 110mg | Sodium: 1033mg | Fiber: 4g | Sugar: 7g

---

This Greek Salad with Grilled Chicken is a delicious and satisfying way to incorporate anti-inflammatory ingredients into your diet. The chicken provides a lean protein source, while the mixed greens, cherry tomatoes, cucumber, red onion, and kalamata olives offer anti-inflammatory properties. Feta cheese adds a tangy and creamy element to the salad, and the homemade dressing is a simple and flavorful complement. This salad can be served as a light lunch or dinner and is easily customized to fit your preferences.

SPINACH SALAD WITH ROASTED BEETS

 15 minutes   45 minutes 🍴 4

Ingredients

For the salad:
- 4 medium-sized beets, peeled and diced
- 2 tbsp olive oil
- 1/2 tsp salt
- 1/4 tsp black pepper
- 6 cups baby spinach
- 1/2 cup chopped walnuts
- 1/4 cup crumbled goat cheese

For the dressing:
- 3 tbsp balsamic vinegar
- 1 tbsp honey
- 1/2 tsp Dijon mustard
- 1/4 cup extra-virgin olive oil
- Salt and black pepper, to taste (optional)

Preparation Steps

- Preheat the oven to 400°F. Toss the diced beets with olive oil, salt, and black pepper, and spread them on a baking sheet.
- Roast the beets for 35-45 minutes until tender and lightly caramelized. Set aside to cool.
- Combine the baby spinach, roasted beets, chopped walnuts, and crumbled goat cheese in a large bowl.
- Whisk together the balsamic vinegar, honey, Dijon mustard, olive oil, salt, and black pepper in a small bowl to make the dressing.
- Drizzle the dressing over the salad and toss to combine.
- Serve immediately.

Calories: 290 kcal | Carbohydrates: 20g | Protein: 7g | Fat: 22g | Saturated Fat: 4g | Cholesterol: 7mg | Sodium: 474mg | Fiber: 4g | Sugar: 15g

This Spinach Salad with Roasted Beets and Walnuts is a nutrient-dense, anti inflammatory meal option. Spinach is rich in vitamins and minerals, while beets offer anti-inflammatory properties and natural sweetness. Walnuts provide a crunchy texture, and heart-healthy fats and goat cheese add a tangy flavor. The balsamic vinaigrette is a simple and flavorful addition that ties the salad together. This salad can be served as a light lunch or dinner and easily modified to suit your preferences, such as adding grilled chicken or swapping out the goat cheese for a vegan cheese alternative.

CAPRESE SALAD WITH BALSAMIC GLAZE

10 minutes   0 minutes   4

Ingredients

- 4 large vine-ripened tomatoes, sliced
- 8 oz fresh mozzarella cheese, sliced
- 1/2 cup fresh basil leaves
- 2 tbsp extra-virgin olive oil
- Salt and black pepper, to taste
- Balsamic glaze for drizzling

Preparation Steps

- Arrange the tomato and mozzarella slices on a large plate or platter.
- Add the fresh basil leaves on top of the tomato and mozzarella slices.
- Drizzle the olive oil over the salad, and season with salt and black pepper to taste.
- Drizzle the balsamic glaze over the salad to taste.
- Serve immediately.

Calories: 253 kcal | Carbohydrates: 5g | Protein: 14g | Fat: 20g | Saturated Fat: 9g | Cholesterol: 45mg | Sodium: 350mg | Fiber: 1g | Sugar: 4g

This Caprese Salad with Balsamic Glaze is a simple and delicious anti-inflammatory salad that can be prepared quickly and easily. Combining fresh tomatoes, creamy mozzarella cheese, and fragrant basil leaves provides a refreshing and nutritious flavor profile. The balsamic glaze adds a sweet and tangy touch to the salad, making it a perfect appetizer or side dish for any occasion. This salad is low in carbohydrates and protein, making it an excellent option for those following a low-carb or ketogenic diet.

CHAPTER 15
SIDES

ROASTED BRUSSELS SPROUTS WITH BACON

10 minutes   30 minutes   4

Ingredients

- 1 lb Brussels sprouts, trimmed and halved
- 4 slices bacon, chopped
- 2 tbsp extra-virgin olive oil
- Salt and black pepper, to taste (optional)
- 2 tbsp balsamic glaze

Preparation Steps

- Preheat oven to 400°F (200°C).
- Toss Brussels sprouts with olive oil, salt, and black pepper in a large bowl until evenly coated.
- Spread Brussels sprouts out in a single layer on a large baking sheet.
- Roast for 20-25 minutes, stirring halfway through until sprouts are tender and lightly browned.
- While the Brussels sprouts are roasting, cook the chopped bacon in a large skillet over medium-high heat until crispy, about 8-10 minutes.
- Once the Brussels sprouts are done roasting, add them to the skillet with the bacon and stir to combine.
- Drizzle the balsamic glaze over the top of the Brussels sprouts and bacon, and stir to coat.
- Serve immediately.

Calories: 190 kcal | Carbohydrates: 10g | Protein: 6g | Fat: 14g | Saturated Fat: 3g | Cholesterol: 15mg | Sodium: 284mg | Fiber: 3g | Sugar: 4g

This Roasted Brussels Sprouts with Bacon and Balsamic Glaze is a flavorful and nutritious anti-inflammatory side dish that is perfect for any meal. The Brussels sprouts are a rich vitamin C and fiber source, while the bacon adds a savory and crispy texture to the dish. The balsamic glaze adds a sweet, tangy touch that complements the dish's flavors. This dish is low in carbohydrates and high in protein, making it an excellent option for those following a low-carb or ketogenic diet.

CAULIFLOWER "RICE" PILAF WITH TURMERIC

10 minutes　　　15 minutes　　　4

Ingredients

- 1 large head of cauliflower, grated or processed into small pieces
- 1 onion, chopped
- 2 cloves garlic, minced
- 1 tbsp grated ginger
- 1 tsp turmeric powder
- 1/2 tsp ground cumin
- 1/4 tsp ground cardamom
- 1/4 tsp ground cinnamon
- 1/4 cup chopped fresh cilantro
- 1/4 cup sliced almonds
- 2 tbsp coconut oil or ghee
- Salt and black pepper, to taste (optional)

Preparation Steps

- In a large skillet, heat coconut oil or ghee over medium heat.
- Add onion and sauté for 3-4 minutes, until softened.
- Add garlic, ginger, turmeric, cumin, cinnamon, and cardamom. Stir to combine and cook for 1-2 minutes, until fragrant.
- Add grated cauliflower to the skillet and stir to coat with the spices.
- Cook for 8-10 minutes, occasionally stirring until the cauliflower is tender but still slightly firm.
- Add chopped cilantro and sliced almonds and stir to combine.
- Season with salt and black pepper to taste.
- Serve hot.

Calories: 120 kcal | Carbohydrates: 8g | Protein: 4g | Fat: 9g | Saturated Fat: 5g | Cholesterol: 0mg | Sodium: 49mg | Fiber: 3g | Sugar: 3g

This Cauliflower "Rice" Pilaf with Turmeric and Ginger is a delicious and nutritious anti-inflammatory side dish for those following a low-carb o ketogenic diet. Cauliflower is an excellent source of fiber, and vitamins C and K, while turmeric and ginger are powerful anti-inflammatory ingredients tha add a warm and aromatic flavor to the dish. This dish is also vegan and gluten free, making it an excellent option for those with dietary restrictions.

SWEET POTATO FRIES WITH CUMIN
10 minutes   25 minutes   4

Ingredients

- 2 large sweet potatoes, peeled and cut into thin strips
- 2 tablespoons olive oil
- 1 teaspoon ground cumin
- 1 teaspoon smoked paprika
- 1/2 teaspoon salt
- Freshly ground black pepper, to taste

Preparation Steps

- Preheat the oven to 425°F (218°C).
- Toss the sweet potato strips with olive oil, cumin, smoked paprika, salt, and black pepper in a large bowl until the sweet potatoes are evenly coated.
- Spread the sweet potato strips in a single layer on a baking sheet.
- Roast the sweet potato fries in the oven for 20-25 minutes, flipping halfway through, until the fries are crispy and golden brown.
- Remove the sweet potato fries from the oven and transfer them to a serving dish.
- Serve hot, and enjoy!

Calories: 163 kcal | Carbohydrates: 23g | Protein: 2g | Fat: 7g | Saturated Fat: 1g | Sodium: 327mg | Fiber: 4g | Sugar: 5g

These sweet potato fries are a great alternative to regular potato fries and have anti-inflammatory benefits. Sweet potatoes are rich in beta-carotene and vitamin C, while cumin and smoked paprika adds delicious flavor and anti-inflammatory properties. These fries are easy to make and can be served as a side dish or a healthy snack.

QUINOA AND KALE STUFFED BELL PEPPERS

15 minutes · 40 minutes · 4

Ingredients

- 4 bell peppers, any color
- 1 cup quinoa, rinsed and drained
- 2 cups vegetable broth
- 1 tablespoon olive oil
- 1 onion, chopped
- 2 garlic cloves, minced
- 1 bunch of kale, stems removed and leaves chopped
- 1 teaspoon dried oregano
- Salt and pepper, to taste (optional)
- 1/2 cup grated Parmesan chees

Preparation Steps

- Preheat the oven to 375°F (190°C).
- Cut off the tops of the bell peppers and remove the seeds and membranes from the inside.
- Bring the quinoa and vegetable broth to a boil in a medium saucepan. Reduce the heat to low, cover, and simmer for 15-20 minutes until the liquid is absorbed and the quinoa is tender.
- In a large skillet, heat the olive oil over medium heat. Add the onion and garlic and sauté until soft and translucent.
- Add the kale to the skillet and sauté until wilted and tender.
- Add the cooked quinoa to the skillet with the kale and onion mixture—season with oregano, salt, and pepper to taste.
- Stuff the bell peppers with the quinoa and kale mixture and place them in a baking dish.
- Bake the stuffed bell peppers in the preheated oven for 20-25 minutes or until the peppers are tender.
- If desired, sprinkle the grated Parmesan cheese over the stuffed bell peppers before serving.

Calories: 255 kcal | Carbohydrates: 40g | Protein: 11g | Fat: 6g | Saturated Fat: 2g | Sodium: 618mg | Fiber: 7g | Sugar: 8g

This quinoa and kale stuffed bell peppers are a delicious, nutritious side dish with anti-inflammatory ingredients. Quinoa is an excellent plant-based protein and fiber source, while kale contains vitamins and minerals. Bell peppers add color and sweetness, making this dish healthy and flavorful. This vegetarian recipe can be made vegan by omitting the Parmesan cheese.

GARLIC AND HERB ROASTED CARROTS

10 minutes   25 minutes   4

Ingredients

- 1 pound carrots, peeled and sliced into even-sized sticks
- 3 cloves garlic, minced
- 1 tablespoon chopped fresh thyme
- 1 tablespoon chopped fresh rosemary
- 2 tablespoons olive oil
- Salt and pepper, to taste (optional)

Preparation Steps

- Preheat the oven to 400°F.
- In a large bowl, combine the carrots, garlic, thyme, rosemary, olive oil, salt, and pepper until well combined.
- Spread the carrot mixture in a single layer on a baking sheet lined with parchment paper.
- Roast in the preheated oven for 20-25 minutes, or until the carrots are tender and golden brown, tossing halfway through cooking.
- Serve hot as a side dish.

Calories: 107 kcal | Carbohydrates: 12g | Protein: 1g | Fat: 7g | Saturated Fat: 1g | Sodium: 78mg | Fiber: 3g | Sugar: 6g

This garlic and herb roasted carrots are a delicious, easy side dish full of anti-inflammatory nutrients. Carrots are a great source of vitamin A and antioxidants, while garlic and herbs like thyme and rosemary have anti-inflammatory and immune-boosting properties. This dish is perfect for a weeknight dinner or holiday meal.

BROCCOLI AND CAULIFLOWER GRATIN

15 minutes   40 minutes   6

Ingredients

- 1 head of broccoli, cut into florets
- 1 head of cauliflower, cut into florets
- 2 tablespoons of olive oil
- 2 cloves of garlic, minced
- 2 tablespoons of flour
- 2 cups of almond milk
- 1/4 cup of nutritional yeast
- 1/4 teaspoon of ground turmeric
- Salt and pepper to taste
- 1/2 cup of gluten-free breadcrumbs

Preparation Steps

- Preheat your oven to 375°F (190°C).
- Blanch the broccoli and cauliflower florets in a large pot of boiling water for 3-4 minutes until slightly tender. Drain and set aside.
- Add olive oil and minced garlic in a saucepan over medium heat. Cook until fragrant for about 1-2 minutes.
- Add the flour and stir continuously for 1-2 minutes to make a roux.
- Gradually whisk in the almond milk and continue stirring until the mixture thickens.
- Add the nutritional yeast, turmeric, salt, and pepper, and continue stirring for another 2-3 minutes until the mixture is smooth and creamy.
- Add the blanched broccoli and cauliflower florets to the saucepan and stir until the florets are coated with the sauce.
- Transfer the mixture to a greased baking dish and sprinkle with the gluten-free breadcrumbs.
- Bake for 20-25 minutes or until the breadcrumbs are golden brown and the vegetables are tender.
- Let cool for a few minutes before serving.

Calories: 310kcal | Carbohydrates: 34g | Protein: 10g | Fat: 16g | Saturated Fat: 4g | Cholesterol: 17mg | Sodium: 299mg | Fiber: 7g | Sugar: 6g

This Broccoli and Cauliflower Gratin is a delicious, healthy side dish with anti-inflammatory ingredients. The combination of broccoli and cauliflower provides a good source of fiber and antioxidants, while the nutritional yeast adds a cheesy and nutty flavor without using dairy. The turmeric in the sauce also provides an anti-inflammatory boost, making this dish a great addition to any meal.

ZUCCHINI NOODLES WITH TOMATO AND BASIL

10 minutes   15 minutes   4

Ingredients

- 4 medium-sized zucchinis, spiralized
- 2 tablespoons olive oil
- 2 garlic cloves, minced
- 2 medium-sized tomatoes, diced
- 1/4 cup fresh basil, chopped
- Salt and pepper, to taste (optional)
- Optional: grated Parmesan cheese for serving

Preparation Steps

- Heat the olive oil in a large skillet over medium-high heat.
- Add the garlic and cook for 1 minute until fragrant.
- Add the zucchini noodles and cook for 2-3 minutes, occasionally stirring, until softened but slightly crunchy.
- Add the diced tomatoes and cook for 2-3 minutes until heated.
- Season with salt and pepper to taste and sprinkle with fresh basil.
- Serve hot, optionally topped with grated Parmesan cheese.

Calories: 89 kcal | Carbohydrates: 7g | Protein: 2g | Fat: 7g | Saturated Fat: 1g | Sodium: 9mg | Fiber: 2g | Sugar: 5g

This zucchini noodles with tomato and basil recipe is a light and refreshing way to enjoy anti-inflammatory veggies. Zucchini noodles provide a low-carb and low-calorie alternative to traditional pasta, while fresh tomatoes and basil add flavor and essential vitamins and minerals. This dish is perfect as a light side dish or as a base for a heartier meal.

BUTTERNUT SQUASH AND APPLE SALAD

20 minutes   25 minutes   4

Ingredients

For the salad:
- 1 medium butternut squash, peeled and cubed
- 2 medium apples, cored and chopped
- 4 cups mixed greens
- 1/4 cup dried cranberries
- 1/4 cup chopped pecans
- Salt and pepper, to taste (optional)

- Olive oil for roasting

For the dressing:
- 1/4 cup olive oil
- 2 tablespoons apple cider vinegar
- 2 tablespoons pure maple syrup
- 1 tablespoon Dijon mustard
- 1 garlic clove, minced
- Salt and pepper, to taste (optional)

Preparation Steps

- Preheat the oven to 400°F (200°C). Line a baking sheet with parchment paper.
- Toss the cubed butternut squash in olive oil, salt, and pepper. Place the squash on the prepared baking sheet and roast for 20-25 minutes until tender and golden brown.
- While the butternut squash is roasting, prepare the dressing by whisking together olive oil, apple cider vinegar, pure maple syrup, dijon mustard, minced garlic, salt, and pepper in a small bowl. Set aside.
- Combine the roasted butternut squash, chopped apples, mixed greens, dried cranberries, and chopped pecans in a large bowl. Drizzle the salad with the dressing and toss gently to coat.
- Serve immediately and enjoy!

Calories: 294 kcal | Carbohydrates: 30g | Protein: 3g | Fat: 20g | Saturated Fat: 3g | Sodium: 166mg | Fiber: 6g | Sugar: 17g

This butternut squash and apple salad with maple dijon dressing is a perfect side dish for fall or winter. Butternut squash is rich in vitamin A and antioxidants, while apples provide a sweet and tangy flavor along with fiber and vitamin C. The maple dijon dressing is a delicious balance of sweet and tangy, adding an extra layer of flavor to the salad. This salad is both satisfying and nutritious and will surely be a crowd-pleaser at any dinner table.

CUCUMBER AND TOMATO SALAD WITH RED ONION

15 minutes   0 minutes   4

Ingredients

For the salad:
- 2 cucumbers, diced
- 4 tomatoes, diced
- 1/2 red onion, thinly sliced
- 1/2 cup crumbled feta cheese
- 2 tablespoons chopped fresh parsley

- Salt and pepper, to taste (optional)

For the dressing:
- 2 tablespoons extra-virgin olive oil
- 1 tablespoon red wine vinegar
- 1 teaspoon Dijon mustard
- 1/2 teaspoon honey
- Salt and pepper, to taste (optional)

Preparation Steps

- Combine the cucumbers, tomatoes, red onion, feta cheese, and parsley in a large bowl.
- Season with salt and pepper to taste.
- Whisk together the olive oil, red wine vinegar, Dijon mustard, honey, salt, and pepper in a small bowl to make the dressing.
- Drizzle the dressing over the salad and toss to combine. Serve chilled.

Calories: 133 kcal | Carbohydrates: 9g | Protein: 4g | Fat: 10g | Saturated Fat: 4g | Cholesterol: 17mg | Sodium: 247mg | Fiber: 2g | Sugar: 5g

This cucumber and tomato salad with red onion and feta is a delicious and refreshing way to incorporate anti-inflammatory veggies into your diet. Cucumbers and tomatoes are low in calories and water content, making them great for hydration. Red onion adds a sharp and tangy flavor, while feta cheese provides a creamy and salty contrast. The simple dressing of olive oil, red wine vinegar, Dijon mustard, and honey brings everything together. Serve this salad as a side dish for a light and healthy meal.

ROASTED BEET SALAD WITH GOAT CHEESE

15 minutes   1 hour   4

Ingredients

For the salad:
- 4 medium-sized beets, washed and trimmed
- 4 cups mixed greens
- 1/2 cup crumbled goat cheese
- 1/2 cup shelled pistachios

For the dressing:
- 1/4 cup balsamic vinegar
- 1/4 cup extra virgin olive oil
- 1 tablespoon Dijon mustard
- 1 tablespoon honey
- Salt and pepper, to taste (optional)

Preparation Steps

- Preheat the oven to 400°F (200°C). Wrap the beets individually in foil and place them on a baking sheet. Roast in the oven for 50-60 minutes or until the beets are tender when pierced with a knife. Let the beets cool, then peel and slice them into wedges.
- Whisk together the balsamic vinegar, olive oil, Dijon mustard, honey, salt, and pepper in a small bowl until well combined.
- Combine the mixed greens, roasted beet wedges, crumbled goat cheese, and shelled pistachios in a large bowl. Drizzle with the dressing and toss to combine. Season with additional salt and pepper, if needed.
- Divide the salad among four plates and serve immediately.

Calories: 292 kcal | Carbohydrates: 18g | Protein: 8g | Fat: 23g | Saturated Fat: 6g | Cholesterol: 13mg | Sodium: 282mg | Fiber: 4g | Sugar: 12g

This roasted beet salad with goat cheese and pistachios is a delicious way to incorporate anti-inflammatory ingredients into your diet. Beets are rich in antioxidants and other beneficial compounds, while goat cheese provides protein and healthy fats. Pistachios add a satisfying crunch and a boost of heart-healthy monounsaturated and polyunsaturated fats. This salad is perfect as a side dish or a light meal.

CONCLUSION

As we come to the end of this book, let's take a moment to reflect on the key points that we have covered. Inflammation is a normal response of the immune system to protect the body from infections and injuries. However, when inflammation lasts long, it can cause several long-term diseases. Adopting an anti-inflammatory lifestyle, including an anti-inflammatory diet, supplements, and lifestyle changes, can help reduce inflammation and improve our overall health.

We explored the benefits of an anti-inflammatory diet, including whole, nutrient-dense foods rich in anti-inflammatory nutrients, such as omega-3 fatty acids, antioxidants, and fiber. We also discussed the importance of avoiding processed foods that cause inflammation, like sugar, trans fats, and refined carbohydrates.

We also discussed the science behind anti-inflammatory foods and how they can help reduce inflammation and prevent chronic diseases. We also provided a 7-day meal plan and 100 delicious recipes to help you get started with an anti-inflammatory diet.

Supplements can also play a role in reducing inflammation and promoting overall health, but it's essential to use them wisely and with caution. We talked about the health benefits of different anti-inflammatory supplements, when and how to use them, and any possible warnings and precautions.

We also talked about changes to your lifestyle, such as less stress, better sleep, and more exercise, that can help reduce inflammation. We discussed the importance of stress reduction and better sleep for overall health and provided tips and strategies to help you manage stress and improve your sleep quality. We also discussed the importance of regular exercise for reducing inflammation and improving overall health.

In conclusion, an anti-inflammatory lifestyle can help reduce inflammation, improve health, and decrease the risk of chronic diseases. The key is incorporating whole, nutrient-dense foods, supplements, and lifestyle changes into our daily routines. It may seem daunting initially, but small changes can make a big difference in the long run. Remember, you can take control of your health and make choices that will benefit you for years.

I encourage you to keep working toward a life that doesn't cause inflammation by looking into the resources in this book. Many excellent books, articles, and websites can provide additional information and guidance.

Thank you for joining me on this journey toward better health. I wish you all the best on your path toward an anti-inflammatory lifestyle.

AFTERTHOUGHT

As the author of this book, I want to express my gratitude for the opportunity to share my knowledge and passion for the anti-inflammatory lifestyle with you. I believe that our health is our greatest asset, and by adopting an anti-inflammatory diet and lifestyle, we can protect and enhance our well-being.

Throughout this book, I've shared evidence-based information on the science behind inflammation, the role of diet in reducing inflammation, the benefits of anti-inflammatory foods, and lifestyle changes that can support an anti-inflammatory lifestyle. I hope the practical tips, meal plans, and recipes in this book will empower you to take control of your health and lead a more vibrant life.

Adopting a new diet and lifestyle can be challenging, but I encourage you to take it one step at a time. Start by making small changes and gradually build up to a more anti-inflammatory lifestyle. Remember, every healthy choice is a step in the right direction.

Thank you for taking the time to read this book and your commitment to your health. I hope the information has been helpful, and I wish you all the best on your journey toward an anti-inflammatory lifestyle.

SHARE YOUR THOUGHTS

Reviews are essential for authors to reach a broader audience and help potential readers understand the value of a book. If you enjoyed reading this book and found it helpful in improving your health and lifestyle, please take a moment to leave a review on Amazon. Your review will encourage the author to continue creating valuable content and help other readers make an informed decision about whether or not to purchase this book.

Writing a review is quick and easy. Log in to your Amazon account, find the book, and scroll to the "Write a customer review" button. You can share your thoughts on what you liked about the book, how it helped you, and any suggestions you may have for the author.

Leaving a review may seem like a small gesture, but it can significantly impact a book's success. Your words could inspire others to read this book and make positive changes. So please take a moment to leave a review and help spread the message of an anti-inflammatory lifestyle.

RECIPE INDEX

REFERENCES

1. Axe, Josh. "10 Anti-Inflammatory Foods You Need to Include in Your Diet." Dr. Axe, 5 Sept. 2018, https://draxe.com/nutrition/anti-inflammatory-foods/.

2. "Anti-Inflammatory Diet: What to Eat to Reduce Inflammation." Healthline, 29 Nov. 2019, https://www.healthline.com/nutrition/anti-inflammatory-diet-101.

3. Bhupathiraju, Shilpa N., et al. "Quantity and Variety in Fruit and Vegetable Intake and Risk of Coronary Heart Disease." American Journal of Clinical Nutrition, vol. 98, no. 6, 2013, pp. 1514–1523. Crossref, doi:10.3945/ajcn.113.066381.

4. Calder, Philip C. "Omega-3 Fatty Acids and Inflammatory Processes." Nutrients, vol. 2, no. 3, 2010, pp. 355–374. Crossref, doi:10.3390/nu2030355.

5. "Chronic Inflammation: Definition, Causes, and Symptoms." Medical News Today, 18 Dec. 2017, https://www.medicalnewstoday.com/articles/248423.

6. Cleveland Clinic. "Anti-Inflammatory Diet." Cleveland Clinic, 2021, https://my.clevelandclinic.org/health/articles/17350-anti-inflammatory-diet.

7. "Fiber and Heart Health." Harvard T.H. Chan School of Public Health, 12 May 2020, https://www.hsph.harvard.edu/nutritionsource/carbohydrates/fiber/.

8. "Foods That Fight Inflammation." Harvard Health Publishing, 2019, https://www.health.harvard.edu/staying-healthy/foods-that-fight-inflammation.

9. "Healthy Sleep Tips." National Sleep Foundation, https://www.sleepfoundation.org/articles/healthy-sleep-tips.

10. Kim, Youjin, and Jung-Hwan Kim. "Ginger Alleviates Obesity-Related Inflammation via Regulating Macrophage Polarization and Inflammatory Gene Expression in Adipose Tissue." Molecules, vol. 26, no. 3, 2021, p. 789. Crossref, doi:10.3390/molecules26030789.

11. Kresser, Chris. "The Top 15 Anti-Inflammatory Foods - Plus, Anti-Inflammatory Diet Tips." Kresser Institute, 12 Aug. 2019, https://kresserinstitute.com/top-15-anti-inflammatory-foods/.

12. Mahajan, Aarti, et al. "Anti-Inflammatory Effects of Curcumin in Recent Chronic Diseases: A Systematic Review and Meta-Analysis of Randomized Clinical Trials." Current Opinion in Clinical Nutrition and Metabolic Care, vol. 22, no. 1, 2019, pp. 11–18. Crossref, doi:10.1097/MCO.0000000000000527.

13. "Nonsteroidal Anti-Inflammatory Drugs (NSAIDs)." Mayo Clinic, 2019, https://www.mayoclinic.org/diseases-conditions/osteoarthritis/in-depth/nsaids/art-20046797.

14. Ornish, Dean. "Can Healthy Eating Reverse Some Cancers?" TEDx Talks, 2015, https://www.ted.com/talks/dean_ornish_can_lifestyle_changes_reverse_some_cancers.

15. Chilton, Floyd. "Dietary Guide to Fighting Inflammation and Aging." Nutrition Today, vol. 51, no. 5, 2016, pp. 231-237. doi: 10.1097/NT.0000000000000167

Printed in Great Britain
by Amazon

23557591R00079